Catharsis
in Healing,
Ritual,
and Drama

Seeing too much sadness
    hath congealed your blood,
And melancholy
    is the nurse of frenzy.
Therefore they thought it good
    you hear a play
And frame your mind
    to mirth and merriment,
Which bars a thousand harms
    and lengthens life.

Induction, scene 2,
    The Taming of the Shrew

Catharsis in Healing, Ritual, and Drama

T. J. Scheff

UNIVERSITY OF CALIFORNIA PRESS
Berkeley · Los Angeles · London

University of California Press
Berkeley and Los Angeles, California

University of California Press, Ltd.
London, England

Library of Congress Catalog Card Number: 78-57314
Printed in the United States of America

1 2 3 4 5 6 7 8 9

For my children, Karl, Robin, and Julie,
who helped me understand grief, fear, and joy

Contents

Contents

Preface

Although the chapters in this book are self-contained, and understandable in themselves, it will probably give most readers background to know the history of the development of my interest in emotions. About nine years ago, after a decade of research on mental hospitals, I became convinced by the flaws I saw in existing programs that any system of treatment would be incomplete if it were based entirely upon professional therapists. Such a system, I thought, would need to be augmented by the development of a large group of lay therapists. These therapists would be trained and supervised by professionals. I had in mind relatively brief, simple training and supervision. My thought was that lay therapists could deal with many of the most frequently occurring types of emotional crises. Under these conditions, mental health professionals could be used as specialists, particularly as trainers and supervisors, and as therapists only for complex, difficult, or intractable cases.

My first step in investigating the issue of lay therapists was to become attached to a lay therapy program called the

Santa Barbara Night Counseling Center. At this center, laypersons provided counseling at little or no charge. They were supervised by mental health professionals, who reviewed cases with them nightly. The basic technique which the counselors were urged to use was attentive listening. However, as part of the program, all counselors were required to attend monthly workshops, in which different therapeutic approaches were demonstrated by local and visiting experts.

As a result of my experiences as a supervisor, and because of my attendance at various workshops, I became convinced that my understanding of psychological therapy, and of the problems of lay and professional therapists, would be incomplete unless I myself participated in at least several therapeutic experiences. My first involvement was with one of the techniques I had seen demonstrated in the Night Counseling Center: Reevaluation Counseling (RC), which has its basic emphasis on catharsis. The procedure requires two meetings a week: a three-hour class, with a teacher and some twenty students, and a two-hour meeting between pairs of the students. This latter meeting is called "co-counseling". In co-counseling, the students try out the techniques that they have learned in class on each other. Each student takes one hour as client, and then, reversing roles, one hour as therapist. Part of each class meeting is devoted to a review of the co-counseling experience by the teacher. Each student gets the experience of being client and counselor, and of being supervised in each role. The foremost goal in all meetings, both in the class and in co-counseling, is emotional discharge.

At the time I had no interest in, or understanding of, emotional discharge, but I found the other major feature of RC, co-counseling, very appealing in terms of my interest in developing lay counselors. Here is a technique, I reasoned, which teaches laypersons how to become both clients and therapists. It seemed to me at the time, and still does, that learning to be a client would help one to be a better therapist, and vice versa. In addition the students might make personal therapeutic gains which would, of course, also be helpful in producing effective therapists. If it proved to be effective, such a program would seem to be ideal for developing a large core of lay therapists.

For three years I immersed myself in therapy. I continued in classes for that time and added co-counseling sessions in addition to those required by the class. I also participated in numerous week-long and weekend workshops, some twenty in all. Finally, I obtained one-way, individual therapy to supplement my class and co-counseling experiences.

During this period I also acted as a counselor, under the supervision of a professional psychotherapist. I obtained a license to be a therapist in the State of California (the license is called Marriage, Family, and Child Counselor) and I began to lead RC classes and to do one-way individual counseling. During this period, which also lasted about three years, I continued to participate in classes and workshops, on a reduced scale, and I gave classes and workshops, as well as one-way counseling, in California, Washington, Sweden, and England.

My personal experience in therapy, and the observations that I made of other participants, both fellow students in the classes I attended, and my own students and clients in my role as therapist, raised several questions in my mind. I noted that this form of therapy caused profound changes in myself and in some of the other participants. The proportions of students and clients affected this way seemed to be about the same: roughly one-third of the participants had dramatic cathartic experiences and showed significant improvements in their orientations and behavior. For the majority of the participants, however, there was little or no change. Most of the persons in this group seemed to enjoy themselves. Many gained rewards other than catharsis and therapeutic change: social contact, intellectual understanding, romance, or friendships, among other things. Occasionally there would be an individual who hated the experience or was temporarily upset by it, perhaps one or two persons among each 100 participants.

These observations led me to look at other forms of therapy. I next spent two years as a participant in a Gestalt group, led by an extremely experienced and skilled leader. In this group, it seemed to me, the success rate was higher; perhaps 50 or 60 percent of the participants underwent cathartic or other therapeutic experiences. It seemed to me, however, that these experiences and the resultant changes were usually of smaller magnitude than those that I saw occurring in RC. My impression was that the number and precision of the therapeutic techniques available in Gestalt was far greater than those in RC, but there was much less follow-up on the successes that were gained. In particular, the idea of repeated catharsis on the same material (see the discussion in Chapter 2), which was emphasized in RC, was totally absent in Gestalt, and this difference in policy resulted in smaller changes in Gestalt participants. My conclusion was that a therapeutic program which combined the use of the manifold and subtle Gestalt techniques with the RC procedure of repeatedly working through the same materials would be more effective than either approach alone.

After my Gestalt experience, I also tried, for relatively brief periods of time, some of the bodily oriented therapies: Bioenergetics, rolfing, and the Alexander method. Although I could see how these techniques could be useful in specific cases, none of them seemed to me to have the power and the wide applicability of the RC and Gestalt approaches.

Another result of my participation in these various forms of therapy was an intellectual and professional interest in what for me was a new area, the social psychology of emotions. How could one explain the powerful changes that I observed in myself and in others? To what extent do similar processes occur outside of therapy? As a sociologist, I was particularly interested in knowing if one might be able to generalize about processes that occurred with individuals in therapy, to the community or societal level. These questions led me to the analysis of social institutions in which collective catharsis sometimes occurs: ritual and drama.

Finally, another intellectual interest grew out of my experiences with therapy: the question of the scientific status of phenomena I had observed. To what extent has the effect of catharsis been systematically documented? This question led me to examine the relevant literature, which is reported in the first two parts of this book (particularly in Chapter 4), and to conduct the studies reported in the last part.

This book represents a blending of two kinds of knowledge: the personal and intuitive knowledge I gained as a participant and as a leader or counselor in therapeutic settings, on the one hand, and the systematic knowledge I have gained through reading the scientific literature and through experience in conducting controlled studies, on the other. In the actual writing of this book, I have found it difficult to achieve an exact balance between the two kinds of knowledge. As it turned out, the tone varies considerably between the three parts, reflecting the difficulty in integrating the different types of knowledge. In Part 3, which reports several systematic studies I conducted, along with possible problems for future research, the emphasis is upon scientific knowledge. Chapters 2 and 3, in Part I, although somewhat less formal, also emphasize the scientific approach. Part II, in which I use my approach to catharsis to analyze social and psychological aspects of drama and ritual, is more intuitive in style.

Finally, in Chapter 3 of Part I, in which I outline my approach to catharsis, I try to achieve a balance between the two styles. As the reader will note, the attempt to maintain a balance between the role of the participant and the role of the observer, which is perhaps the central subject of the book, may also be reflected, to some extent, in the varied forms my writing takes.

Acknowledgments

My wife, Jane Hewitt Scheff, contributed substantially to the development of Chapter 6 and made helpful suggestions on many of the other chapters. Edward Gross, Christopher Jencks, and Michael P. Nichols also read a draft manuscript and made helpful suggestions. The following persons commented on, or contributed to, particular chapters:

Preface:	Aaron Cicourel and Susan Parrish
Chapter 2:	Janie Spencer
Chapter 3:	Arlie Hochschild, Robert I. Levy, Robert Michels, Stephen C. Scheele
Chapter 5:	Donald R. Cressey, Arlie Hochschild, Nancy Jurik, Robert I. Levy. Don D. Bushnell and Stephen C. Scheele contributed research assistance.
Chapter 6:	Russell Astley, Arlene Daniels, Irwin Deutscher, Erving Goffman, Lorraine Hatch, Maynard Mack, and Mark Rose
Chapter 7:	Jeffrey H. Goldstein, Gary I. Schulman, A. Robert Sherman, and William Bielby
Chapter 8:	Jonathan Turner

Acknowledgments

Chapters 1–4, 7, and 8 were written especially for this book. One part of Chapter 5 was published as "The Distancing of Emotion in Ritual," in *Current Anthropology* 18 (Sept. 1977) 483–505; a somewhat shorter version of Chapter 6 has been published as "Audience Awareness and Catharsis in Drama" in *Psychoanalytic Review* 63 (1976) 529–554.

I. Theory

1.

Introduction: Emotions and Catharsis

Emotions play very little part in most theories of social behavior. They are either omitted entirely or, at best, treated as an undifferentiated residue. Marx and his followers do not deal with emotions in any explicit way; the main components of Marxian theory are basic drives, such as hunger and the need for shelter, economic considerations of profit and loss, and the relentless movement of capital and technology.

Most sociological theories include emotions as a component, but only as a residual category. The students of collective behavior, beginning with Durkheim, Tarde, and LeBon, were quite concerned about the emotions of crowds, but they made no attempt to describe differences in the emotional responses of crowds, or the effects of these differences. These theorists tended to see emotions as antisocial and irrational. This bias is quite clear in Weber, who makes the assumption that action based on emotion is not rational.

Although Mead sought to include states of the body, such as emotions, in his social psychology, he gives them so little attention that they are, in effect, ignored. Mead

3

was primarily concerned with the human capacity for rational thought. He considers the self to be the process of dialogue between the "I," the biological impulses of the body, and the "me," the social processes that the individual has internalized. Involuntary emotional responses such as grief, fear, rage, and shame are not excluded from Mead's scheme, since they could be considered as part of the "I." But Mead seldom deals with emotions as examples of the "I"; his usual illustrations use simple drives like hunger. Most of Mead's discussion concerns the "me," the organization of social forms that is incorporated by the individual, and the part played by the "me" in gaining self-control and the capacity for rational thought and behavior. Working in the Meadian tradition, Shibutani's (1961) approach to sentiments comes closest to being an exception to the strictures above. He gives sentiments an important, indeed, central, place in his theory and carefully differentiates the major types. Although there is some overlap, his conception of sentiments does not emphasize some of the most important properties of emotions that are discussed here.

Parsons' treatment of emotions in his theory of social action is similar to Mead's. Although affective orientations are assigned a place among the pattern variables that could, potentially, play a central role in the theory, their importance is never developed. Like Durkheim, Weber, and Mead, Parsons makes little attempt to differentiate among the various emotions. For this reason, their place in the theory remains ambiguous.

A critique of Weber's concept of social action that is applicable to all of the major theories of society has been offered by Hochschild (1975, 284–85).

Weber confuses irrationality, as it refers to *behavior* with irrationality as it refers to a feeling. He posits a model of social

4

action that is *rational,* while action based on emotion, like action based on ignorance or tradition, is non-rational. I see two problems with this—a confusion between rationality and emotionlessness, and the implication that emotions and feelings are not positively required by the rational action of individuals and smooth functioning of institutions in everyday life. Weber thought emotions important, and deplored a 'rationalistic bias' that might grow out of what he meant merely as a methodological device. But I do not get the sense that he saw how necessary emotions were, not to messing things up but in making them run.

Let us take his example of a theoretically posited course of rational action on the stock market. He proposes to examine deviations from rational behavior as something a sociologist might explain in terms of "irrational emotions" (e.g., panic). But the difference (in terms of feeling and emotion) between the normal stock market and the sudden depression in stocks is the difference between one affective state of stockbrokers and *another* affective state. It is highly questionable whether emotion enters into the life of stockbrokers *only* when there is panic, that emotion makes people act *only* irrationally. Surely emotion and sentiment are active ingredients in rational behavior as well. A normal day at the stock market, not simply during a panic, would amply show that feelings of satisfaction, excitement, anxiety, anguish and glee, are all part of a good (rational) day's work. Weber mistakes actual emotionlessness for the prevailing norm of affective neutrality we suppose stockbrokers have internalized. If all stockbrokers were to stop caring about what seems like colorless stock prices and to experience "the rat race" as no more meaningful than anything else, the stock market would deviate from what it would be under conditions of *normal emotionality.*

The point that Hochschild makes is an important one; emotions are not, as Weber and most of the other theorists assumed, alien to society but are an intrinsic and necessary part. If we accept this argument, there would seem to be a great need for more theories which acknowledge the importance of emotions, not only in nonrational behavior but in rational behavior as well.

A starting point for an interdisciplinary approach to

emotion is provided by Ruth Benedict in *Patterns of Culture* (1934). Benedict's work is no longer held in high esteem, not because it is not valuable, but because the particular rubrics she used are considered obsolete. In the three societies that she discussed in *Patterns of Culture,* she sought to find what she called "the dominant character" or "the ruling motivation" of each culture. She typified the Zuni culture as Apollonian and the Dobu and Kwakiutl as Dionysian. (She borrowed these terms from Nietzsche, who saw those aspects of human nature representing reason and order as Apollonian and those representing mystery and chaos as Dionysian.) In terms of the work currently being done in social science, this kind of analysis seems much too global and tendentious. It is now difficult to find agreement on any aspect of an entire culture, much less its dominant character or ruling motivation.

I would argue, however, that the value of Benedict's analysis does not depend on the summary labels she used. Her analysis rather is concerned with the relationship among three elementary components of human experience: feeling, thought, and action. In each culture she looked for the way in which thought and feeling were related to each other and to action. In the Zuni culture, she found innumerable instances in which feeling was suppressed so that behavior was controlled by conscious thought. In most of the Zuni culture, she argued, behavior was controlled by thought at the expense of feeling. As an example, we can take her description of a Zuni mourning ritual. On the fourth *day* after death, the bereaved are told by the chief that it has now been four *years* since the death of their kin: "The chief speaks to the people telling them that they shall not remember any more, 'It is now four years he is dead'. . . time has lapsed to free them of grief. The people are dismissed and the mourning is over" (p. 101).

In the other two societies, the Dobu and the Kwakiutl, Benedict found the equation usually reversed. Behavior was dominated by feeling at the expense of thought. In Dobu society, critical events in human life were thought to be the result of sorcery and witchcraft—members of the society lived in fear and suspicion of their fellows. In Benedict's interpretation, the beliefs and practices in this society were such that fear was continually being generated. Members of the society believed in and therefore practiced sorcery, which gave rise to more fear, which strengthened their beliefs and practices, and so on. In this society, according to Benedict, its members not only felt fear, but wallowed in it. There were few arrangements for using thought to dispel fear or remove its basis.

Her analysis of the Kwakiutl was similar. She argued that the members of this society continually explored the single emotion of humiliation, either by humiliating others or being humiliated themselves. For example, in the potlatch ceremony, a member of the society could go to extravagant lengths to show his wealth by destroying or giving away his own property. Embarrassment or humiliation was not merely felt by members of this society but was indulged to its utmost. As with the Dobu, rational thought was allowed to play little part in Kwakiutl social arrangements. The society provided mechanisms for runaway orgies of humiliation.

The utility of Benedict's work need not rest, therefore, on claims of typifying a whole culture or finding its dominant character. An integrated approach to emotion can be based on the concrete analysis of the relationship of feeling to thought and action, at any level of analysis, in any given setting or institution within a society. Furthermore, we need not claim that the relationship among feeling, thought, and action constitutes the dominant character of a society, but merely that it is an important aspect which should be investigated.

Benedict's analysis may be used for a rudimentary interpretation of the absence of treatments of emotion in theories of social behavior. Social theorists may be considered as belonging to the Zuni-like culture of scholars. Such cultures select persons who have repressed their emotions in the service of intellectual goals and develop norms and procedures which maintain the dominance of intellect over feeling. Scholarly theories of the human experience which exclude emotions are both products and causes of repression.

Emotion Work

An analysis that is more concrete than Benedict's, but still has the same spirit, is suggested by Arlie Hochschild's concept, "emotion work."[1] Hochschild has discussed some of the ways in which people do work on their emotions, either seeking to summon emotions which are not present or trying to suppress emotions which are. For example, a mourner at a funeral may struggle to produce feelings of grief, just as a bride or groom may strive to feel happy. Hochschild defines emotion work as "the awareness of manipulating attitudes, thoughts, or behaviors in the service of changing feelings."

The present analysis will broaden the definition of emotion work in two ways. First, I include under the heading of emotion work both aware activities of suppressing or inducing feeling, and those of which the actor has little or no awareness. Second, I include not only those activities in which the individual works on his own emotions, with

1. Arlie Hochschild. *Sex Differences in the Culture of Emotion: A Study of the Relation Between Self and Feeling.* Unpublished manuscript. In this study, Hochschild does a content analysis of written protocols in which students describe some of their emotional experiences. She shows that there is a relationship between the amount of emotion work that individuals report and their sex, religious and class backgrounds, and other status variables.

which Hochschild's research deals, but also similar activities by *others*. By this definition, emotion work would be "manipulating attitudes, thoughts, or behaviors in the service of changing one's own feelings or those of others."

Given this broad definition, emotion work may occur not only within the individual, but also at the interpersonal and societal levels. For example, let us return to Benedict's observation about how the Zuni shortened the mourning period. When the chief tells the mourner that four years have passed, he is doing emotion work not so much on himself but on the mourner, that is, the emotion work is interpersonal. To the extent that the mourner believes or pretends to believe the fiction that four years have passed, he is doing work on his own emotions. Finally, to the extent that the entire community participates in the fiction, emotion work is occurring at the societal level. In these terms, one may say that the characteristic emotion work in the Zuni culture by the individual and/or by those around him is to suppress all emotion, just as the characteristic emotion work in both of the Dionysian cultures is to evoke a single one—in the Dobu, fear, in the Kwakiutl, humiliation.

It is convenient to divide emotion work into two major domains; socialization and interaction. There has been considerable discussion of the process that we are referring to as emotion work in the literature on the socialization of emotions. The best conceptualization of this area is that of Silvan Tomkins, particularly in his work on the socialization of crying (1963, II, Chap. 15). Tomkins argues that in modern societies the socialization of emotions is primarily through punishment. Children are systematically and regularly punished for crying and screaming, to the point that individuals come to suppress their own grief. In terms of our earlier discussion, we would expect that the punitive socialization of emotions would lead to recurring situations of the Apollonian type, in which action is controlled by thought, with emotion suppressed.

The second major domain of emotion work is social interaction. Representative is the analysis by Erving Goffman under the heading of "impression management" (1959; 1974, 570–572). A close reading of his work shows that much of the content of impression management involves control of emotional expression, either suppressing unwanted emotions or evoking desirable ones. Important empirical work is represented by the studies of Paul Ekman, et al, on the expression of the emotions in the face, and studies of emotional leakage and deception (1969, 1972).

The concept of emotion work can be seen to be very useful in that it subsumes some of the major processes that are considered in the literature on emotion and feeling. However, there is one respect in which this analysis is incomplete. There is a strong tendency in modern social science and psychology to treat emotion as if it were completely a cultural product. In this conception, emotion has no real biological function—its manifestations are to be completely understood in terms of learning. Emotional processes are a product of emotion work, whether at the personal, interpersonal, or societal level. Particularly in psychology, the increasing dominance of learning theory formulations has led most researchers to either ignore emotions or to treat them as epiphenomena. Crying behavior, for example, is understood solely in terms of conditioning: if crying is positively reinforced, it will continue, if negatively conditioned, it will be extinguished. If crying is extinguished, few learning theorists would even raise the issue of the long-range effects that not crying might have.

Even Tomkins, who above all other theorists is most

concerned with integrating learning and psychodynamic theory, is somewhat ambiguous on this point. He begins his analysis of anguish by asking a simple question: "Why do we seldom see an adult cry?" He notes that suffering is ubiquitous and that crying is the principal expression of suffering, yet most adults rarely cry. The answer he suggests is that adults learn substitutes for crying—whole repertories of actions which may serve as equivalents to crying. For example:

> . . . the adult who sits in the dentist's chair and attempts not to cry out in pain commonly braces himself against this innate affective display by a substitute cry which is emitted in advance of the pain. He may tightly squeeze the sides of the dental chair with both hands, or tighten the muscles of his stomach and diaphragm or tightly curl his toes and feet. He senses that if these muscles are in a stage of massive contraction before and during the experience of pain this will help to drain off the massive motor discharges of the cry and interfere with the innate contractions of the diaphragm and vocal cords which would normally constitute the cry of distress. Whether by interference or substitution this enables the individual to cry as it were in his hands, or feet, or diaphragm, and not to cry in his face and throat (Tomkins, II, 59).

What is not clear about this passage, and in the other examples that Tomkins gives, is whether the various substitutes for crying which Tomkins discusses are exact equivalents for crying, that is, whether substitution has any short- or long-term effects. In some passages at least, he seems to suggest that substitution, in some cases, may have no effects.

This book is based on an alternative premise: that emotional expressions such as crying are biological necessities. Crying itself is instinctual; the baby comes out of the womb with the ability to cry. This ability is unlearned. What is learned is the ability to suppress crying. I will argue that the suppression of crying and other cathartic processes, which is learned, has supremely important consequences, both for persons and societies. I will now introduce the idea of catharsis.

Catharsis

Not all social scientists have limited their analyses to emotion work. There is more than a hint in Durkheim's treatment of social organization that there is a specific "social emotion" and that this emotion has enabling, as well as limiting, effects on human abilities. This thread is not altogether absent from more recent treatments of collective behavior, particularly in the work of Blumer (1946), in his conceptualization of expressive, as opposed to acting, crowds. The thread has been lost, however, in most contemporary theories of collective behavior, as in the work of Turner and Killian (1957), or Smelser (1963). For these theorists, the expressive behavior of crowds is an evanescent phase in the development of an acting crowd.

I would like to introduce the idea of catharsis in two different ways. First I will describe a class of seeming exceptions to a theory of motivation that is widely held, the pleasure-pain theory of motivation. Second, I will provide three case histories as examples of the process of catharsis. Finally, this chapter will provide a brief history of the idea of catharsis, in addition to summarizing the contents of the book as whole.

It is commonly believed that most people are motivated by the desire to experience pleasure and to avoid pain. Even admitting that this scheme is too simple, it is still serviceable enough to explain much of the behavior that is observable in ourselves and others. There is a class of behavior, however, which seems to constitute a glaring exception to the pleasure-pain theory, which might be called "thrill-seeking" behavior. Why do children ride on roller coasters and enjoy ghost stories? Why do adults pay to see horror movies? All three of these activities involve the seeking out of stimuli which result in the emotion of fear, which is ordinarily seen as a distressful or painful emotion. What about the enormous audience for dramas involving unrequited love or loss, for example, the daytime serials on TV and the romantic novels that are referred to as "tear-jerkers"? People who seek stimuli which provoke fear or grief seem to be contradicting the commonsense principle that avoiding pain is a primary motive in human behavior. The theory of catharsis that will be described here seeks to explain this seemingly paradoxical behavior.

To state it in a very brief and simplified form, the theory of catharsis argues that thrill-seeking is an attempt to relive, and therefore resolve, earlier painful experiences which were unfinished. When we cry over the fate of Romeo and Juliet, we are reliving our own personal experiences of overwhelming loss, but under new and less severe conditions. The experience of vicarious loss, in a properly designed drama, is sufficiently distressful to awaken the old distress. It is also sufficiently vicarious, however, so that the emotion does not feel overwhelming. The balance between distress and security, which I will refer to as distancing, will be a central theme in this book. I will argue that cathartic crying, laughing, and other emotional processes occur when an unresolved emotional distress is reawakened in a properly distanced context.

This theory is applied to three different topics: psychotherapy, ritual, and drama. In the area of psychotherapy, I attempt to answer the question of the basic curative process. My hypothesis is that catharsis is a necessary condition for therapeutic change. In the area of ritual, I raise a question concerning the poverty of modern ritual. I argue that most rituals in modern society are over-distanced, that is, they are too vicarious, and therefore do not lead to catharsis. The formula for successful ritual, I

13

argue, is the same as that for successful drama: the social form must reawaken collectively held distress which is unresolved in everyday life. The reawakening must occur in a context which is sufficiently safe so that the distress is not experienced as overwhelming. Under these conditions, catharsis occurs.

The theory of catharsis further argues that unresolved emotional distress gives rise to rigid or neurotic patterns of behavior and that catharsis dissipates these patterns. These ideas are illustrated in the following case history. (I have made some slight changes in both this case and the others that follow, in order to insure the anonymity of the subjects.)

The subject was a self-employed engineer who was a member in a group I led. He was raised to be a "real man," i.e., to be strong and silent. His business was a moderate success, but he was tense in his dealing with his associates and family. He was subject to severe and frequently recurring bouts of migraine and hyperacidity. Between the ages of sixteen and forty, he had cried only once, and was somewhat unexpressive of other emotions as well.

At the age of forty, he was separated from his wife and children after a marriage which had lasted many years. After two months of separation, feeling intensely lonely and missing his children, the subject began seeing a psychiatrist for an hour a week. He told the psychiatrist his feelings, and felt some relief but was still tense and lonely.

During this period, the subject had attended his first psychotherapy group. The group emphasized catharsis of emotions. In the class, he had told the story of his childhood to a fellow participant. He had also stood up before the class and repeated phrases provided by the leader, "I hurt," and "I hurt a little bit." This last phrase she had had him repeat several times, first in a normal voice, then falsetto, then in a basso voice. The subject felt a lump in his throat during this episode, but no other feelings. There were several episodes of crying by other participants at various points in the class. The subject remembers feeling envious of the participants who were crying. After the class, which occupied almost the whole day, the subject went swimming and had dinner. At some point during this period after the class, he noticed a new sensation in his upper abdominal area, which felt like a knot the size of his fist. It was not particularly painful or even unpleasant, but it persisted for the rest of the day.

In the evening, he went to the home of a friend. He told her about the group he had attended in the afternoon. When repeating the phrases he had spoken in front of the class, he began crying. At first the crying was very tense and somewhat painful: he felt bitter and strained. The sensation was brittle and difficult, like the dry heaves. After some fifteen or twenty minutes, the crying became more relaxed. After another quarter hour of relaxed crying, he stopped and lay back to rest.

After a few minutes' rest, the subject began to shake and sweat. The shaking was violent, like an earthquake. Yet he felt no fear. The sensation, rather, was not unpleasant. He felt that he was in touch with an enormous source of energy, like surfriding a twenty-foot wave. He also expressed the feeling another way: like being shaken by the neck by a giant. After some thirty minutes of shaking, it stopped as suddenly as it had begun. The subject felt refreshed and relaxed. He noticed that the knot in his stomach was getting smaller.

After another brief rest, the subject began to feel angry. He started shouting and cursing and moving on the bed. His writhing became so violent that he fell out of bed. On the floor, he continued cursing, and began chewing on the rug. At this point, a peculiar thing happened. He sensed that his friend was becoming upset, so he stopped what he was doing, and said to her: "Are you all right?" She said, "Don't worry, I'm all right." He then immediately went back to the anger, without any pause whatsoever. He had no sense of what he was angry about, but it seemed to be there, ready for him to express it, as if there had been no interruption at all. After some thirty minutes, it seemed to pass. He got back in bed.

Once again, he rested. Because of what had happened before, he anticipated further strong emotional responses. After a few minutes, he felt a strong sensation again, this time the urge to laugh. He laughed a deep, relaxed laugh. He began repeating a phrase that had occurred to him: "I believe, Lord, oh help me to believe." The subject reported that the laughter felt so deep and powerful that he felt almost like someone else was laughing through him. With the laughter, he felt strongly exhilarated.

After a half hour of laughing, he felt finished. He lay back and rested. The knot in his stomach had disappeared.

In the morning, when the subject awoke, he began crying again. He remembers repeating a line of Auden's poetry, "All over Europe, the nurses were itching to boil their children." He went on to go through the whole cycle of discharge again, shaking, screaming, and laughing, but in a much shorter space of time, fifteen or twenty minutes all told. He dressed to catch a plane. At breakfast, he realized that he felt quite different than he had before. He felt full of energy, and his senses felt exquisitely sharp, especially his sense of smell and taste. The sound of music on the radio was unbelievably beautiful. The smell and taste of breakfast was delightful. The subject felt that he had never actually tasted orange juice before, as if he could taste each molecule.

At the airport, he chanced to meet a friend who was on the same flight. He told his friend about his experience. After deplaning, while entering the terminal building, the subject felt the emotions coming up again. This time he felt it would be inappropriate, and he sought to keep the emotions from coming. He told his friend what was happening, then took ten or twenty deep breaths, and the anticipated catharsis did not occur.

After this the subject experienced himself as having changed in fundamental ways. He felt much more relaxed and open, and less driven. Although he hadn't realized that they were deficient, after the catharsis his senses seemed sharper, especially his sense of smell, to the point where he felt that he hadn't been sensing before the change. His work habits changed. He felt more creative and less driven. He realized in retrospect that he had been obsessed with work, and had let other aspects of his life take second place. He continued to work, but he felt he had more perspective and was more effective. Finally, he felt more effective and open with people. The impatience and frustration that he often felt seemed virtually to disappear.

Although the subject continued to cry and yawn, the experience of a massive catharsis occurred only one more time, about six months after the first. On this occasion, the subject was in a situation in which his life was endangered. He had a fit of fear, much like the shaking episode in the first catharsis, but even more violent. After some fifteen minutes of the most intense shaking and sweating, but again without the experience of fear, the subject got up from the floor, completely refreshed. He reported that his mind seemed utterly clear. He gave a public speech soon after, extempore, which he thought was the most effective speech he had ever given. He reported that the words seemed to be there when he needed them, without planning or forethought.

For about a year after the first massive discharge, the subject cried almost daily. This period of crying was ended by a series of violent arguments with his former wife, which occurred for several weeks about twelve months after the initial discharge. At the end of this period, the crying stopped completely for several months. When the crying resumed, it was much lighter and more frequent than it had been before the initial abreaction but less frequent and more painful than it had been during the year of crying. Nevertheless, the subject felt that his behavior had been permanently changed by the experience.

Most of the changes had continued three years afterwards. The psychosomatic disturbances did not disappear completely but became infrequent and mild. The subject also reported that obsession with work diminished almost to the vanishing point. His final observation was that before catharsis, he spent most of his time feeling neither pleasure nor pain, but suspended. After catharsis, and to the present, he reported considerable variation, with many highs and lows, including one or two days a month of mild depression.

I have reported this case in detail because it highlights in a dramatic way some central features of the cathartic process. Particularly noticeable is the association between emotional inexpressiveness and rigidity in the years preceding catharsis and the association of relaxation, heightened sensory experience, and increased flexibility following catharsis. This case is quite unusual in the massive and condensed form that catharsis took. In most of the other cases I am familiar with, the discharge processes took place over a long period and in a less dramatic form. This case is typical in one way, however: As massive as the discharge experiences were, they were apparently not complete. The subject had little awareness of the sources of the emotional distress involved in the cathartic process, and the rigid patterns of behavior and the psychosomatic disturbances did not terminate completely. In fact, a new, postcathartic symptom—mild depression—occurred.

In my experience, a complete ending of symptoms on the basis of catharsis is extremely rare. During my involvement in thousands of hours of cathartic therapy, it occurred only once. The subject, whom I will call Will, was twenty-five. He complained of hallucinations when he came to me for therapy. He had been diagnosed as schizophrenic and was unable to hold even a dishwasher's job because of the recurrence of his symptoms. I spent some sixty hours with Will both in individual and group therapy. After approximately three months of treatment, Will had a massive experience of fear discharge. He was a "guest" in a nonprofessional halfway house for the mentally ill, which my students had established. I was the consultant. One evening after supper he began to shake and sweat. He asked to be held. All four of us present held Will as he shook violently for some twenty minutes. Several minutes after he had stopped shaking, I noticed that he was sitting by himself, looking at a wall, and smiling happily, as if he were watching television. When I asked him what he was doing, he said that he was seeing scenes from his childhood, as in a movie. He said they were so real that they might have been happening again. He also said that some of the scenes that he would have expected to be frightening were not. After a half hour spent in this way, Will announced that he had remembered his childhood, much of it for the first time, and that he was cured. During the three subsequent months, when I was able to keep in touch with Will, he had no recurrence of symptoms. Apparently a dramatic cure had been effected by catharsis alone.

The following case illustrates some of the difficulties

encountered in connection with catharsis. (As before, I have altered some details to protect the subject's anonymity.) It is not exactly a treatment failure, since the subject was not in treatment:

I was interviewing Ralph for research purposes. He was a thirty-seven-year-old physician. I had heard through a friend that he had had a substantial cathartic experience, so I arranged an interview with him. About five years before the interview, he had cried for several hours. Since he hadn't cried for years, it was a dramatic event. It occurred on Christmas day after he, his wife, and two children had watched the TV film "Mr. Roberts." He realized, after the long cry, that the actor Henry Fonda, who was the lead, reminded him of his father. The circumstances on that day were strained, since he was planning to leave his wife. His father had been killed during World War II under circumstances similar to the death of Mr. Roberts in the film. Ralph was ten at the time of his father's death. He did not cry or mourn and denied death. "He'll come back."

Ralph had seen "Mr. Roberts" the year before, but it did not affect him. The second viewing took place under conditions which increased the impact of the film, since (he realized afterwards) he identified with his own ten-year-old, who was shortly to lose his father (through divorce), as he had lost his father through death, when he was ten. As Ralph described the episode, he became tearful during the interview. He finally broke down and wept. I found that he would continue the crying after he stopped if I had him say the phrase "poor boy." After having wept for some twenty minutes, Ralph made connections for the first time between his father's death and his own present behavior. He explained that he was very feisty, to the point that he got into many fights. He had recently gotten into a fight in a bar, breaking a man's jaw with a bottle. Because of this episode, Ralph was being sued for damages. The fight had occurred in December. Ralph now saw a connection: "November and December are difficult times for me; I am erratic still. I don't give a shit. If it's gonna happen, it'll happen." His father was killed in November, and his birthday was one day later than the day of his death. His own birthday was in December.

I asked him if he had become less feisty after the cry five years ago. He said that he had for a while, perhaps a year, but that he was now as feisty as ever. I suggested that he might want to work through his father's death. To my surprise, he rejected the idea. He said he was embarrassed by his crying and had no intention of dealing with the subject any further. So far as I know from my limited later contact with him, he did no further crying.

Ralph's case illustrates several features of the theory of catharsis: the connection between failure to mourn, denial of death, and repression. Later, after the initial catharsis, the subject recalled the forgotten events. The link between male violence and the repression of grief is also suggested. Finally, the subject's refusal to follow up on this episode illustrates one of the barriers to catharsis.

Unfortunately, most cases of catharsis are not nearly so clear-cut. The impediments to catharsis, as well as the conditions in which it occurs, and the effects of repression and catharsis are more usually subtle and complex. In the discussion that follows I will outline a scheme of interpretation that may help to deal with these issues. It should be remembered that the comment offered here is provisional, since the subject matter is vast and poorly researched. I hope that the reader will understand and take what I have to say as work in progress, rather than as a definitive statement.

The Current Status of the Theory of Catharsis

The value of catharsis has been the subject of intensely heated controversy for more than 2,000 years. Responding to Plato's condemnation of drama for arousing the passions, and thereby undermining the State, Aristotle contended that drama may produce catharsis by purging the audience of pity and terror (Aristotle, 1968; Wimsatt and Brooks, 1969). Judging from the deluge of commentary, Aristotle's statement on the nature and function of catharsis is probably the most controversial sentence ever written (Lain Entralgo, 1970, 183–239).

The debate over catharsis has continued to the present

day, in several different contexts. The argument between the advocates of catharsis, on the one hand, and the advocates of insight, on the other, has been a central issue almost from the beginning of psychotherapy. Freud, with his collaborator Breuer, at first advanced a treatment based on catharsis (Freud and Breuer, 1895). In his later work, Freud abandoned cathartic techniques to develop psychoanalysis, in which emphasis is placed on conscious insight. This episode will be further discussed in the next chapter. In contemporary psychotherapy, the controversy continues, with some types of therapies, such as Gestalt, Bioenergetics, and Primal Therapy, emphasizing catharsis, and others, like Psychoanalysis and Behavior Modification, suggesting that catharsis provides little if any benefit.

In their analyses of the social functions of ritual, anthropologists have long been involved in a similar dispute. Malinowski (1945), representing the positive orientation toward catharsis, argued that ritual served an important function in that it alleviated the anxieties of the participants in areas of uncertainty. Other anthropologists, however, denied the cathartic function of ritual. Radcliffe-Brown (1952), for example, answered that it was just as reasonable to assume that ritual created emotional distress, as it was to assume that it alleviated it. Other anthropologists, like Evans-Pritchard (1965), concurred. In recent years, catharsis has lost its central position among students of ritual. In contemporary anthropology, the emphasis has shifted away from catharsis to a concern for cognitive and symbolic functions (Lévi-Strauss, 1969; Douglas, 1970; Turner, 1967). A similar movement has occurred in psychotherapy and psychology. Once of central importance, the idea of catharsis is now considered passé by most researchers in social science, psychology, and psychiatry.

The purpose of this book is to argue that the closing of

the debate over catharsis has been premature. The theory of catharsis has never been adequately tested, in order to determine whether it should be retained or discarded, either because of a lack of careful definition of what constitutes catharsis or because of a lack of systematic data to evaluate the theory. The absence of an adequate test of the theory can be shown in each of the various debates.

In psychotherapy, the majority of psychoanalysts uncritically accepted Freud's criticisms of catharsis, even though they are brief and casual, compared to his careful documentation of the effectiveness of catharsis in *Studies on Hysteria*. Neither Freud nor any other psychotherapist provided any systematic evidence showing that catharsis was ineffective. The one study that has been done suggests the opposite, that catharsis is by far the most frequent cause of success in psychotherapy (Symonds, 1954). In recent years, the success of a cathartic technique for treating pathological bereavement, called "regrief therapy," provides strong clinical evidence for the validity of the theory (Volkan, 1975).

As in psychotherapy, the dispute over the function of catharsis in ritual has proceeded without systematic evidence. Radcliffe-Brown and Evans-Pritchard pointed out that Malinowski had no real evidence to support his hypothesis that ritual alleviated anxiety, which was true. However, it was equally true that Radcliffe-Brown and Evans-Pritchard also had no data themselves to contradict the hypothesis. Like the argument between Plato and Aristotle over drama, and between early and late Freud over psychotherapy, the argument over the functions of ritual was a strictly theoretical disputation.

The same cannot be said about the debate over "aggression catharsis" in experimental social psychology. Berkowitz (1962), Feshback and Singer (1971), and many, many others have produced a large body of systematic research about the effects of aggression and vicarious aggression on subsequent levels of hostility.

In his review of studies both of actual and of vicarious aggression, Quanty (1976) concludes that the weight of evidence goes against the hypothesis of catharsis. Among three reviews of vicarious aggression, there are disparate conclusions. Liebert and Schwartzberg (1977) state that the weight of evidence suggests that the viewing of vicarious violence leads to increased violence, but Kaplan and Singer (1976) conclude that the results are so faulty or ambiguous that no conclusions can be drawn. The third reviewer, Geen (1976), is more cautious in drawing definite conclusions, but agrees more with Liebert and Schwartzberg than with Kaplan and Singer, suggesting that results of existing studies support social learning theory more than the catharsis hypothesis.

The problem with these studies is certainly not the lack of systematic data. The problem, rather, is the lack of a conceptual definition of what constitutes catharsis. Berkowitz and others have tested the hypothesis that catharsis occurs through aggressive *behavior*. In a typical study, he has shown that active retaliation against an aggressor not only does not lower the level of hostility of the person who is retaliating but may actually raise it. Although this seems to be an important finding, its relevance to the theory of catharsis is limited. Neither Aristotle's doctrine nor Freud and Breuer's technique defines catharsis in terms of behavior. Both dramatic and psychotherapeutic theories involve the reexperiencing of past emotional crises in a context of complete security: in the safety of the theatre or the therapist's office. Catharsis in these contexts is analogous to Wordsworth's definition of poetry—emotion recollected in tranquillity. The extension of catharsis to include aggressive retaliation seems unwarranted.

Studies of vicarious aggression appear more relevant to

the theory of catharsis, especially studies of the effects of viewing television violence, since the contexts studied are similar to dramatic or psychotherapeutic settings envisioned by theorists of catharsis. Even in these studies, however, there are two serious conceptual problems. First, the treatment variable in studies of the effects of television is the *viewing* of dramatic violence. However, it is probably a mistake to equate the process of catharsis with the stimuli which may cause it to occur. Presumably catharsis involves a particular type of emotional response within the individual. The viewing of dramatic violence may or may not give rise to this response, depending on the characteristics of the stimuli, the viewers, and other conditions.

Feshback and Singer were able to show that high school students who viewed violent TV fare committed fewer aggressive acts than those students who didn't view it, a phenomenon presumably demonstrating the effects of catharsis. The correlation they found, however, was weak. According to our theory, if the researchers had had some way of separating the viewers of violent fare into those who experienced a cathartic emotional response, such as laughter, from those who didn't, the data would have shown still stronger support for the theory of catharsis. Among the viewers of violent fare who experienced catharsis, the drop in aggressive behavior would have been greater than the amount reported in the study. Among the viewers of violent fare who did not experience a cathartic response, there would have been no reduction of aggressive behavior at all, thus isolating the causative process: the occurrence of a cathartic response in the context of viewing violent TV fare. The theory of catharsis would be more amenable to testing if catharsis were defined independently of the arousing stimuli.

The second issue concerns distancing. Most studies of the effects of viewing violence rate only the quantity of violence, not the quality. For example, some studies include comic and cartoon violence, others arbitrarily exclude it. I would argue that most comic violence is properly distanced, and should therefore lead to catharsis, and that more realistic violence in drama is underdistanced, and would not have cathartic effects. (This argument is continued in Chapter 5.) Until some control over distancing of the stimulus materials is introduced, it will be difficult to interpret the relation of most studies of vicarious aggression to the catharsis hypothesis.

These remarks suggest that the theory of catharsis might provide a powerful framework for research on psychotherapy, ritual, and the effects of drama, if the theory could be stated clearly enough to allow empirical testing. This book seeks to formulate a clearly defined theory of catharsis, show its application to the study of ritual and drama, and present some empirical studies which support it. In the next chapter, the development of the original cathartic theory by Freud and Breuer is reviewed. The third chapter contains a statement of the new theory of catharsis that I propose. Chapter 4 summarizes the state of evidence with respect to the theory of catharsis. Part II contains two chapters which apply the concepts of repression, distancing, and catharsis to the analysis of ritual and entertainment. Chapter 5 concerns the distancing of emotion in ritual and mass entertainment, and Chapter 6 examines the part that distancing and catharsis play in classical drama, with special emphasis on Shakespeare's plays. Part III is oriented toward the application of the ideas discussed here to research. Chapter 7 reports a study of the relationship between humor and tension. The last chapter concludes with a statement of propositions involved in the theory of catharsis, along with suggestions for future research.

2.

Freud and Breuer's *Studies on Hysteria:* A Reassessment

The history of the modern theory of catharsis begins in 1880 with the treatment of a patient by Josef Breuer, a physician in Vienna. "Anna O." was twenty-one, and she presented numerous and severe symptoms. Freud describes her case in this way:

Her illness lasted for over two years, and in the course of it she developed a series of physical and psychological disturbances which decidedly deserved to be taken seriously. She suffered from a rigid paralysis, accompanied by loss of sensation in both extremities on the right side of her body, and the same trouble from time to time affected her on her left side. Her eye movements were disturbed and her power of vision was subject to numerous restrictions. She had difficulties over the posture of her head; she had a severe nervous cough. She had an aversion to taking nourishment, and on one occasion she was for several weeks unable to drink in spite of a tormenting thirst. Her powers of speech were reduced, even to the point of her being unable to speak or understand her native language. Finally, she was subject to conditions . . . of confusion, of delirium, and of alteration of her whole personality . . . (Freud, 1910, 10).

What is one to make of this massive list of symptoms?

Surely the patient is suffering from some soon-to-be fatal brain injury or disease. Breuer, since he found no indication of organic disease, and since he noted that the patient had recently gone through an emotional crisis in which she had nursed her father through the illness which led to his death, diagnosed the case as one of hysteria, as would most other physicians. Such a diagnosis brought some assurance to the physician, in the sense that at least it was quite unlikely that such a disorder would prove fatal, which would be a likely first impression. However, at the time, the diagnosis of hysteria meant little else, since its cause and treatment were completely unknown.

In fact, at the time, and to some extent still today, the diagnosis of hysteria often decreased the likelihood that the patient would receive any help from the physician. Freud explained the situation in this way:

Thus the recognition of the illness as hysteria makes little difference to the patient, but to the doctor quite the reverse. It is noticeable that his attitude towards hysterical patients is quite other than towards sufferers from organic disease. He does not have the same sympathy for the former as for the latter: for the hysteric's ailment is in fact far less serious and yet it seems to claim to be regarded as equally so. And there is a further factor at work. Through his studies, the doctor has learned many things that remain a sealed book to the layman: he has been able to form ideas on the causes of illness and on the changes it brings about—e.g., in the brain of a person suffering from apoplexy or from a malignant growth—ideas which must to some degree meet the case, since they allow him to understand the details of the illness. But all his knowledge—his training in anatomy, in physiology and in pathology—leaves him in the lurch when he is confronted by the details of hysterical phenomena. He cannot understand hysteria, and in the face of it he is himself a layman. This is not a pleasant situation for anyone who as a rule sets so much store by his knowledge. So it comes about that hysterical patients forfeit his sympathy. He regards them as people who are transgressing the laws of his science—like heretics in the eyes of the orthodox. He attributes every kind of wickedness to them, accuses them of exaggeration, of deliberate deceit, of malingering. And he punishes them by withdrawing his interest from them (ibid., 11–12).

With Breuer, however, this was not the case. Even though he had not the slightest idea of what to do, he sought to help the patient in any way he could. His helpfulness was quickly rewarded.

Anna O. turned out to be an extraordinary patient. According to Jones, Freud's biographer, it was she who ". . . was the real discoverer of the cathartic method . . ." (Jones, 1953, 223n., cf. also 244n.). Breuer's description of the case is consonant with Jones's statement:

I have already described the astonishing fact that from beginning to end of the illness all the [symptoms] . . . were permanently removed by being given verbal utterance in hypnosis, and I have only to add an assurance that this was not an invention of mine which I imposed on the patient by suggestion. *It took me completely by surprise,* and not until symptoms had been got rid of in this way in a whole series of instances did I develop a therapeutic technique out of it (Freud and Breuer, 1895, 81–82). (my italics)

An example of Anna's technique is provided by Breuer:

It was in the summer during a period of extreme heat, and the patient was suffering very badly from thirst; for, without being able to account for it in any way, she suddenly found it impossible to drink. She would take up the glass of water that she longed for, but as soon as it touched her lips she would push it away like someone suffering from hydrophobia. As she did this, she was obviously in an *absence* [dissociated state, TJS] for a couple of seconds. She lived only on fruit, such as melons, etc., so as to lessen her tormenting thirst. This had lasted for some six weeks, when one day during hypnosis she grumbled about her English "lady-companion," whom she did not care for, and went on to describe, with every sign of disgust, how she had once gone into this lady's room and how her little dog—horrid creature!—had drunk out of a glass there. The patient had said nothing, as she had wanted to be polite. After giving further energetic expression to the anger she had held back, she asked for something to drink, drank a large quantity of water without any difficulty, and awoke from her hypnosis with the glass at her lips, and thereupon the disturbance vanished, never to return (ibid., 69).

Freud comments on the importance of Anna's discovery:

Never before had anyone removed a hysterical symptom by such a method or had thus gained so deep an insight into its causation. It could not fail to prove a momentous discovery if the [patient's other symptoms] . . . had arisen and could be removed in this way (Freud, 1910, 13–14).

Breuer quickly learned to use Anna's discovery and soon demonstrated that all of Anna's symptoms could be dealt with using the same technique:

Each individual symptom in this complicated case was taken separately in hand; all the occasions on which it had appeared were described in reverse order, starting before the time when the patient became bedridden and going back to the event which had led to its first appearance (Freud and Breuer, 1895, 70).

The technique was exacting and laborious, since some of the symptoms involved the recollection of numerous occurrences. (Anna remembered 293 instances of not hearing before this symptom was removed!) (Freud and Breuer, 1895, 71). After two years of such treatment, the culminating event was reached, which brought an end to the most persistent symptom, the paralysis of Anna's right arm:

On the last day—by the help of rearranging the room so as to resemble her father's sickroom—she reproduced the terrifying hallucination which constituted the root of her whole illness . . . (ibid., 64).

Note the innovation of rearranging the room to bring back the situation of her father's illness and death, thus inducing the "terrifying hallucination," which Breuer describes as follows:

In July 1880, while he was in the country, her father fell seriously ill of a subpleural abscess. Anna shared the duties of nursing him with her mother. She once woke up during the night in great anxiety about the patient, who was in a high fever, and she was under the strain of expecting the arrival of a surgeon from Vienna who was to operate. Her mother had gone away for a short time and Anna was sitting at the bedside with her right arm over the back of her chair. She fell into a waking dream and saw a black snake coming towards the sick man from the wall to bite him. . . . She tried to keep the snake off, but it was as though she was paralyzed. Her right arm, over the back of the chair, had gone to sleep and had become anaesthetic and paretic; and when she looked at it the fingers turned into little snakes with death's heads (the nails). . . . When the snake vanished, in her terror she tried to pray. But language failed her: she could find no tongue in which to speak, till at last she thought of some children's verses in English and then found herself able to think and pray in that language. The whistle of the train that was bringing the doctor whom she expected broke the spell (ibid., 73).

After Anna had relived this dream, the paralysis of her right arm, which had lasted two years, and her inability to speak German, her native tongue, vanished. Breuer terminated treatment. He did not claim that she was completely cured at this point:

After this (the end of treatment) she left Vienna and traveled for a while, but it was a considerable time before she regained her mental balance entirely. Since then she has enjoyed complete health (ibid., 76).

Freud and Breuer do claim that the use of the cathartic method, in the case of Anna O. and the other cases described in *Studies on Hysteria,* uncovered the causes and removed all of the major symptoms, and that they had therefore discovered the cause and cure of hysteria.

Before considering Freud's cathartic theory and method further, we will describe the other cases in *Studies on Hysteria.* All of the cases were women, and, with the exception of Anna O., they were all Freud's patients. There are five cases presented as separate chapters: Anna, Emmy, Lucy, Katrina, and Elisabeth, and fragments of four other cases dispersed throughout the book: Cäcilie, Mathilde, Rosalia, and the "highly gifted lady." Five of the women were young (eighteen to twenty-four) and unmarried, the other four older (thirty to forty) and married. A few of the social characteristics of the patients can be deduced from the case histories: Lucy was an English governess, Emmy von N. and Elisabeth von R. appear to have been aristocrats. Katrina was the daughter of the owner of an Alpine hotel. Since we know Anna's identity, as will be discussed below, we know that she was middle-class and Jewish.

The symptoms of these patients range in severity from those that were extremely incapacitating (Anna, Cäcilie, Elisabeth, and Emmy); moderate (Katrina and Mathilde); mild (Lucy and Rosalia); and, finally, to a case in which there were no symptoms or incapacitation, the highly gifted lady, who seems to have been a widowed housewife, whom Freud says he was acquainted with, who was not a patient at all.

Anna's symptoms have already been described. Freud does not describe all of Cäcilie's symptoms, but it is clear that, like Anna's, they were numerous and severe, including trigeminal neuralgia (violent headaches), which lasted from five to ten days and occurred two or three times a year (Freud and Breuer, 1895, 218).

Emmy also had a very large number of symptoms which caused impairment: phobias, hallucinations, pain, cramping and paralysis, and facial and verbal tics. Elisabeth's symptoms were much more localized but also impairing: she had pain and partial paralysis in her right leg. The two patients with moderate impairment had fewer symptoms: Katrina had anxiety attacks, and Mathilde was depressed. The patients with mild symptoms had little incapacitation, as symptoms occurred only in restricted circumstances. Lucy hallucinated a particular odor, and

Rosalia, who was training to be a singer, complained of a feeling of choking and constriction at times during her singing.

In the eight cases who were patients (excluding, therefore, the highly gifted lady), there was only one treatment failure: Emmy. As we shall see below, this was the first case in which Freud attempted to use the cathartic method he had heard about from Breuer. As Freud repeatedly acknowledged, he was not able to use the method correctly, since he was still using the method of hypnotic suggestion.

This was my first attempt at handling [cathartic technique]. I was still far from having mastered it; in fact I did not carry the analysis of symptoms far enough, nor pursue it systematically enough . . . (Freud and Breuer, 1895, 83). I was completely under the sway of Bernheim's book on suggestion . . . (ibid., 113).

In this case, rather than let Emmy experience her distresses and discharge them, Freud sought to eliminate them through hypnotic and posthypnotic suggestion.

This case should not be counted as a failure of the cathartic method. Two more cases are ambiguous. Rosalia's treatment was incomplete (213), and in the case of Katrina, who was treated under the most informal circumstances in the Alps, there was no possibility of follow-up. In the remaining five cases, however, the treatment was unambiguously successful. As we will see below, Anna O. went on to a career of extraordinary eminence. The symptoms of Cäcilie, as far as they are described, were removed one by one. Mathilde and Lucy were completely cured. The case of Elisabeth must have been particularly gratifying to Freud. Although the treatment was broken off by the patient, who felt that Freud had betrayed a confidence to her mother, within two months he heard from a colleague that she was completely free of her symptom: the impairment of her ability to walk due to pain in her right leg, which had persisted for two years before the beginning of treatment. Freud ends the case description on a note of restrained triumph:

In the spring of 1894 (two years after the end of treatment) I heard that she was going to a private ball for which I was able to get an invitation, and I did not allow the opportunity to escape me of seeing my former patient whirl past in a lively dance (Freud and Breuer, 1895, 201).

Theory and Technique

On the basis of his experience with these cases, Freud believed that the cause of hysteria began with a violent emotional shock:

In traumatic neuroses the operative cause of the illness is not the trifling physical injury but the affect of fright—the psychical trauma. In an analogous manner, our investigations reveal, for many, if not for most, hysterical symptoms, precipitating causes which can only be described as psychical traumas. Any experience which calls up distressing affects—such as those of fright, anxiety, shame or physical pain—may operate as a trauma of this kind (ibid., 40).

Hysterical symptoms, as Freud repeated in a later formulation, were "residues—precipitates, they might be called —of emotional experiences" (Freud, 1910, 14). However, emotional shock was only a necessary, but not a sufficient, cause for hysteria. In addition, there must have been circumstances which prevented the emotion from being expressed. In the cases of his early patients, Freud noted that nursing relatives was often such a circumstance:

Anyone whose mind is taken up by the hundred and one tasks of sick-nursing which follow one another in endless succession over a period of weeks and months will, on the one hand, adopt a habit of supressing every sign of his own emotion, and on the other, will soon divert his attention away from his own impressions, since he has neither time nor strength to do justice to them. Thus he will accumulate a mass of impressions which are capable of affect, which are hardly sufficiently perceived and which, in any case, have not been weakened by abreaction (ibid., 202-203).

Any situation which impeded the expression of negative emotions, as in nursing, or in the case of Katrina, embarrassment over her father's incestuous sexual advances, or any other impediment to spontaneous emotional expression, can result in neurosis.

Events are traumatic to the extent that, first, they result in powerful negative emotions and, second, to the extent that these emotions have been retained, and not discharged. Freud goes on to indicate a third feature of the causes of neurosis: that traumatic events are virtually always part of a series, rather than single occasions:

In the case of common hysteria it not infrequently happens that, instead of a single, major trauma, we find a number of partial traumas forming a group of provoking causes. These have only been able to exercise a traumatic effect by summation and they belong together in so far as they are in part components of a single story of suffering (ibid., 40).

Each symptom is associated with a series of events which has its own theme of distress:

. . . there is an unmistakable linear chronological order which obtains within each separate theme. . . . It was as though we were examining a dossier that had been kept in good order (ibid., 333).

Freud referred to these series of events as "the files."

These files form a quite general feature of every analysis and their contents always emerge in a chronological order which is as infallibly trustworthy as the succession of days of the week or names of the month in a mentally normal person (ibid., 334).

The most common traumatic events in the files in these cases concerned loss, either the death of relatives (Anna, Emmy, Elisabeth, and the highly gifted lady) or the breakup of a romance (Lucy, Mathilde, and again Elisabeth). The second most common event in the files is incestuous sexual assault (Katrina and Rosalia). According to Freud, there was also a sexual element in the case of Anna O. which Breuer was unaware of (Freud and Breuer, 1895, fn. 75–76; Jones, 1953, I, 246 ff.) In the case of Cäcilie, there is a third kind of event, involving violent disputes with her husband. For convenience, a summary chart of the case characteristics is included.

It is important to note that the traumatic events which constitute the files are almost entirely forgotten by the pa-

Outline of Cases in Freud and Breuer, *Studies on Hysteria*

Page	Number/Name	Dates	Age	"Cause"	Treatment	Outcome	Symptoms
Complete Cases							
55-82	1. *Anna O.*	1880-82	21	Loss (death of father)	Catharsis	Cure	Severe
83-143	2. *Emmy von N.*	1888 or 89	40	Loss (death of husband)	Catharsis and suggestion	No cure	Severe
175-202	3. *Elisabeth von R.*	1892	24	Loss (death of father)	Catharsis	Cure	Moderate
144-160	4. *Lucy R.*	1892	30	Loss (break-up of romance)	Catharsis	Cure	Mild
Fragments of cases							
105-106, 217-238	5. *Cäcilie*	1889-92	33?	??	Catharsis	Cure?	Severe
164-174	6. *Katrina*		18	Sexual assault (by father)	Catharsis	Cure?	Mild to moderate
203-205	7. *"Highly gifted lady"*		?	Loss (deaths of relatives)	Self-induced catharsis	"Cure"	None
204-205	8. *Mathilde H.*		19	Loss (break-up of romance)	Catharsis	Cure	Moderate
210-215	9. *Rosalie H.*		23	Sexual assault (by father)	Catharsis	No cure	Mild

tient. Furthermore, when one or more of the memories associated with them is touched upon, the patient is apt to resist remembering, in some cases, to resist in a most strong and resourceful way. Freud clearly says that these memories were outside of the patient's conscious awareness: they were unconscious. Because the emotions associated with these memories seem absolutely overwhelming to the patient (Freud speaks of "severely paralyzing affects" [Freud and Breuer, 1895, 45]), the memories have been repressed and are therefore unavailable to the patient under ordinary circumstances.

Breuer had used hypnosis with Anna O. to overcome the forces of repression, and Freud at first copied this technique. By the time he treated Lucy (1892), three years after he began to use the cathartic method, however, he had found that hypnosis was not necessary. Freud states that he "conducted her whole analysis while she was in a state which may in fact have differed very little from a normal one" (Freud and Breuer, 1895, 145). It is also clear that he did not use hypnosis with Elisabeth, or with the case of a woman he treated for anxiety neurosis (Freud and Breuer, 1895, 150–152n.). In both cases, he conducted most of the analysis as a normal conversation. When he came to a point at which the patient seemed to be unable or unwilling to remember, he used a device he learned from Bernheim, that he called "head pressure".

I decided to start from the assumption that my patients knew everything that was of any pathogenic significance and that it was only a question of obliging them to communicate it. Thus when I reached a point at which, after asking a patient some question such as "How long have you had this symptom?" or: "What was its origin?" I was met with the answer "I really don't know," I proceeded as follows. I placed my hand on the patient's forehead or took her head between my hands and said: "You will think of it under the pressure of my hand. At the moment at which I relax my pressure you will see something in front of you or something will come into your head. Catch hold of it. It will be what we are looking for. Well, what have you seen or what has occurred to you? (Freud and Breuer, 1895, 148).

The head-pressure device gave Freud faith that he could conduct an analysis without the use of hypnosis:

On the first occasions on which I made use of this procedure . . . I myself was surprised to find that it yielded me the precise results that I needed. And I can safely say that it has scarcely ever left me in the lurch since then. It has always pointed the way which the analysis should take and has enabled me to carry through every such analysis to an end without the use of somnambulism. Eventually I grew so confident that, if patients answered, "I see nothing" or "Nothing has occurred to me," I could dismiss this as an impossibility and could assure them that they had certainly become aware of what was wanted but had refused to believe that that was so and had rejected it. I told them I was ready to repeat the procedure as often as they liked and they would see the same thing every time. I turned out to be invariably right. The patients had not learned to relax their critical faculty. They had rejected the memory that had come up or the idea that had occurred to them, on the ground that it was unserviceable and an irrelevant interruption, and after they had told it to me it always proved to be what was wanted. Occasionally, when, after three or four pressures, I had at last extracted the information, the patient would reply: "As a matter of fact I knew that the first time, but it was just what I didn't want to say," or "I hoped that would not be it" (ibid., 148–149).

In his later work, Freud became confident that every patient could be taught the method of free assocation, so that even the device of head pressure was not necessary to overcome the forces of repression. By learning, as Freud said, "to relax their critical faculty," and to report *every* thought or image which occurred to them, the patient could follow a trail of associations back to the repressed memories in the file.

The treatment which Freud and Breuer developed was

to have the patient go through her file for each symptom, evoking the traumatic memories one by one. The most significant element in this process was referred to by them as "abreaction," which they defined as follows:

> . . . the whole class of *voluntary and involuntary* reflexes—*from tears to acts of revenge*—in which, as experience shows us, the affects are discharged. If this reaction takes place to a sufficient amount a large part of the affect disappears as a result (ibid., 42). (my italics)

Perhaps realizing that this definition is quite vague, they go on to justify it by reference to common usage:

> Linguistic usage bears witness to this fact of daily observation by such phrases as "to cry oneself out" . . . and to "blow off steam" . . . If the reaction is suppressed, the affect remains attached to the memory. An injury that has been repaid, even if only in words, is recollected quite differently from one that has had to be accepted. Language recognizes this distinction, too, in its mental and physical consequences; it very characteristically describes an injury that has been suffered in silence as "a mortification" . . . . The injured person's reaction to the trauma only exercises a completely "cathartic" effect if it is an *adequate reaction*—as, for instance, revenge. But *language serves as a substitute for action;* by its help, an affect can be "abreacted" almost as effectively. In other cases speaking is itself the adequate reflex, when, for instance, it is a lamentation or giving utterance to a tormenting secret, e.g., *a confession.* If there is no such reaction, whether in deeds or words, or in the mildest cases in tears, any recollection of the event retains its affective tone to begin with (ibid., 42–43). (my italics)

They describe the process of abreaction in the following way:

> For we found, to our great surprise at first, that *each individual hysterical symptom immediately and permanently disappeared when we had succeeded in bringing clearly to light the memory of the event by which it was provoked and in arousing its accompanying affect, and when the patient had described that event in the greatest possible detail and had put the affect into words* (ibid., 40–41).

This formula is somewhat more complicated than it first appears, in that it contains three separate components:

1. A detailed description of the event(s) which provoked the symptom.
2. The physical arousal of the accompanying affect.
3. Describing the affect in words.

They are at pains to point out that abreaction does not occur if one or more of these components are missing, as, for example, in the following passage about affect:

Recollection without affect almost invariably produces no result. The psychical process which originally took place must be repeated as vividly as possible; it must be brought back to its *status nascendi* and then given verbal utterance (ibid., 40).

As we shall see below, Freud and Breuer are manifestly unclear, both in this passage and in their case descriptions, as to what is meant when they say that the original psychic process associated with a trauma must be repeated "as vividly as possible." For the present discussion, it will suffice to say that Freud and Breuer define abreaction as the key element in the cathartic method, even though their conception of abreaction is broad and vague.

To emphasize further the idea that the method is concerned with emotions that have been retained rather than discharged, Freud refers to the curative process as the "abreaction of arrears." Freud uses this term explicity in two of the cases, Mathilde H. and the highly gifted lady, and it is strongly implied by his description of the treatment of Cäcilie M. in terms of "the payment of old debts":

The patient had experienced numerous psychical traumas and had spent many years in a chronic hysteria which was attended by a great variety of manifestations. The causes of all these states of hers were unknown to her and everyone else. Her remarkably well-stocked memory showed the most striking gaps.

She herself complained that it was as though her life was chopped in pieces. *One day an old memory suddenly broke in upon her clear and tangible and with all the freshness of a new sensation.* For nearly three years after this she once again lived through all the traumas of her life—long forgotten, as they seemed to her, and some, indeed, never remembered at all—accompanied by the acutest suffering and by the return of all the symptoms she had ever had. The "old debts" which were thus paid covered a period of *thirty-three years* and made it possible to discover the origins, often very complicated, of all her abnormal states (ibid., 105). (my italics)

The process of the abreaction of arrears is clearest in the case of the highly gifted lady:

She has already nursed to the end three or four of those whom she loved. Each time she reached a state of complete exhaustion, but she did not fall ill after these tragic efforts. Shortly after her patient's death, however, there would begin in her a work of reproduction which once more brought up before her eyes the scenes of illness and death. Every day she would go through each impression once more, *would weep over* it and console herself—at her leisure, one might say. This process of dealing with her impressions was dovetailed into her everyday tasks without the two activities interfering with each other. The whole thing would pass through her mind in chronological sequence (ibid., 203). (my italics)

In addition to the abreaction of arrears after her loved ones' deaths, this patient also did commemorative weeping:

In addition to these outbursts of weeping with which she made up arrears and which followed close upon the fatal termination of the illness, this lady celebrated *annual festivals of remembrance* at the period of her various catastrophes, and on these occasions her vivid visual reproductions and expressions of feeling kept to the date precisely. For instance, on one occasion I found her in tears and asked her sympathetically what had happened that day. She brushed aside my question half-angrily: "Oh no," she said, "it is only that the specialist was here again today and gave us to understand that there was no hope. I had no time to cry about it then." She was referring to the last illness of her husband, who had died three years earlier. I should be very much interested to know whether the scenes which she celebrated at these *annual festivals of remembrance* were always the same ones or whether different details presented themselves for abreaction each time, as I suspect in view of my theory (ibid., 204). (my italics)

The question which Freud raises at the end of this passage, whether the patient was repeatedly weeping over exactly the same scene, turns out to be an extremely important one for the theory of catharsis, as we shall see below. The whole case of the highly gifted lady is also of considerable interest, since it involves a process that might be called self-treatment.

To summarize the argument to this point, Freud and Breuer developed a theory about the causes and treatment of hysteria. They argued that hysteria was caused by the repression of emotional reactions. The cure for hysteria was the abreaction of the arrears; one by one, the patients must discharge the emotions associated with all of the traumatic events in their files.

After several years of using the cathartic method, Freud came to the conclusion that the results he had achieved were not permanent. He then went on to develop psychoanalysis. But Freud's decision to abandon catharsis may well have been erroneous. He reports only one case suggesting that the cathartic cure was not permanent—the case of Anna O.—and he may have misinterpreted that case. Even if there were other, unreported failures, the techniques that Freud and Breuer used may have been at fault, rather than the theory of catharsis. The next chapter will be devoted to assessing possible flaws in the theory and technique that Freud and Breuer used. In the remainder of this chapter, I will consider the evidence that Freud reports on the impermanence of cathartic cures.

Although Freud refers to cases from *Studies on Hysteria* frequently in his later work, virtually none of the references concern the permanence of the cures achieved. In the twenty-four volumes of Freud's collected works, there are hundreds of references to Anna O., Elisabeth R., et al., but almost all of the references concern symptoms or dynamics as reported at the time of the original therapy. In all of these references, there is only one passage concerning long-term outcome. This reference occurs in *A General Introduction to Psychoanalysis,* which is based on a series of lectures given in 1915–17, some thirty years after the period of *Studies on Hysteria:*

Breuer's first patient was *fixated,* . . . to the time when her father was seriously ill and she nursed him. In spite of her recovery, she has remained to some extent cut off from life since that time, for although she has remained healthy and active, she did not take up the normal career of a woman (Freud, 1949, 243).

As it stands, this passage is rather cryptic, or even confusing. On the one hand he says the patient, Anna O., is recovered, and has remained healthy and active. On the other hand, he says she has remained cut off from life, from the normal career of a woman. What does he mean?

As luck would have it, we know Anna O.'s true identity and the details of her subsequent career. Freud's biographer, Jones, discloses that Anna O. was in reality Bertha Pappenheim, who went on to achieve extraordinary eminence:

. . . she became the first social worker in Germany, one of the first in the world. She founded a periodical and several institutes where she trained students. A major part of her life's work was given to women's causes and emancipation, but work for children also ranked high. Among her exploits were several expeditions to Russia, Poland, and Roumania to rescue children whose parents had perished in pogroms (Jones, 1953, 225).

Given such sterling achievements, what could Freud mean when he says that she remained cut off from life, from the normal career of a woman? He must mean only one thing:

it is clear from Jones' report that she didn't marry and have children. Freud's judgment in this case seems to rest on a doctrinal prejudice about the role of women.

Ellenberger offers another analysis of the case of Anna O., which seemingly contradicts my analysis:

Juan Dalma has shown the connection between Anna O.'s cure and the widespread interest in catharsis that followed the publication, in 1880, of a book on the Aristotelian concept of catharsis by Jacob Bernays (the uncle of Freud's future wife.) For a time catharsis was one of the most discussed subjects among scholars and was the current topic of conversation in Viennese salons. No wonder a young lady of high society adopted it as a device for a self-directed cure, but it is ironic that Anna O.'s unsuccessful treatment should have become, for posterity, the prototype of a cathartic cure (Ellenberger, 1970, 484).

There are two ideas in this passage: the first, that Breuer's treatment of Anna O. was a failure, is clear. The second idea is quite ambiguous; Ellenberger intimates that Anna O.'s cure was based on suggestion, since Anna O. may have known of Bernay's theory of catharsis. I will first discuss the idea that the treatment was a failure.

According to Jones, there was a hiatus of several years between Breuer's termination of Anna O.'s treatment and her recovery. This possibility is allowed by Breuer's description of the ending of treatment:

After (the end of treatment) she left Vienna and travelled for a while, but it was a considerable time before she regained her mental balance entirely. Since then she has enjoyed complete health (Freud and Breuer, 1895, 75–76).

According to Jones, however, the hiatus lasted more than a year, and was a time of great distress for Anna. Indeed, she is alleged to have spent part of the year in a mental hospital, and to have become addicted to opiates.

Oddly enough, although Ellenberger argues that Anna's treatment was a failure, he discredits almost all of

Jones's descriptions of Anna's plight during the hiatus. He was unable to find any evidence that Anna had been a patient at the hospital where Jones states she was treated. Furthermore, according to Jones, Anna was either in the hospital or home-bound during most of 1882. Ellenberger finds evidence which seems to contradict Jones on this point also:

> . . . the photograph of Bertha (the original of which the author has seen) bears the date 1882 embossed by the photographer and shows a healthy-looking, sporting woman in a riding habit, in sharp contrast to Breuer's portrait of a home-bound young lady who had no outlet for her physical and mental energies (Ellenberger, 1970, 483).

What is incontestable about Anna is that, whether the hiatus between the end of treatment and recovery was two months or two years, recover she did and that she went on to become a formidable person, a mover and shaper of events. However one interprets the evidence, her case would seem a poor foundation for discrediting cathartic theory.

The same might be said in regard to Ellenberger's second point: since Anna may have known about Bernays' theory of catharsis, her cure might have been based on auto-suggestion. (Actually Ellenberger stops short of this charge, since he acknowledges the reality of unconscious processes.) Even if we accept as proven that she knew Bernays' theory, this fact would not invalidate the cure. Frank (1961) has shown that suggestion is an extremely important factor in all psychotherapeutic success. One might argue that Anna might have had expectations about therapy provided not by the therapist, the usual case, but from another source.

To summarize, I have argued that the evidence upon

which Freud based his judgment that cathartic cures were not permanent now seems unconvincing. In the next chapter, I will present a theory of catharsis which will allow us to assess the adequacy of the techniques that Freud and Breuer used.

3.

A New Theory of Catharsis

At the end of the last chapter, a question was raised about one of the reasons that Freud gave for abandoning the cathartic method. He argued that the results achieved were not permanent, yet gave very little evidence for this conclusion. As was shown, the one case on which his conclusion may have rested, Anna O., is susceptible to an interpretation quite different from Freud's.

This chapter will be devoted to another reason that Freud's rejection of the cathartic method may have been premature. Suppose, for the sake of argument, that Freud's assessment of the transiency of his cathartic cures was completely correct. It is still possible that the difficulties Freud and Breuer encountered were not due to the invalidity of the theory but to flaws in the techniques they used. The theory that Freud and Breuer stated was crude and, in crucial ways, quite vague. I will argue that their techniques, which followed from the theory as they formulated it, were faulty, even though the basic theory is essentially valid.

To make this point, it will be necessary to outline a new theory of catharsis, as a framework for assessing

Freud and Breuer's work. At the heart of the theory of catharsis is the process of emotional discharge which brings relief to emotional tension. Freud and Breuer called this process abreaction, and defined it, as indicated earlier, as: " . . . the whole class of voluntary and involuntary reflexes—from tears to acts of revenge—in which, as experience shows us, the affects are discharged" (Freud and Breuer, 1895, 42). For research purposes, this definition is hopelessly vague. What kinds of reflexes? What are their external and subjective signs? It is also extremely broad, including both complex voluntary actions ("revenge") and simple involuntary processes ("tears"). If we turn to other cathartic therapies for guidance, there is even less help. In Primal Therapy, the basic discharge process, which is called a primal, is defined very simply as "a total feeling-thought experience from the past" (Janov, 1970, 86). There is no attempt to classify the kinds of feelings involved, or the distinguishing marks which differentiate primals from other kinds of emotional processes. Surprisingly, most of the other therapies are equally vague as to what constitutes catharsis; no definition is given in the theories of Bioenergetics, Reichian therapy, Gestalt, or any of the other major cathartic therapies.

The most important idea in Freud and Breuer's definition of catharsis is that it is a reflex—an unlearned, involuntary, and ultimately instinctive, internal bodily process, like the example that Freud gives of crying. This concept narrows the range of possible definitions of catharsis considerably, eliminating, for example, all voluntary and overt behaviors, such as revenge. The question is what *specific* reflexes are cathartic? Sneezing, vomiting, and orgasm are all reflexes, but they are not cathartic, that is, they do not resolve emotional tension. Grief, fear, anger, and embarrassment are usually considered to be the major emotional tensions. Are there additional emotions that

47

should be included? Furthermore, what are the marks of the catharsis of these emotions, in the same sense that crying is usually taken to signal the discharge of grief? These are difficult questions, since, as indicated, earlier discussions of catharsis provide no guidance.

What is needed is a provisional definition of the reflexes that constitute catharsis. Such a definition would allow us to state the theory of catharsis as a series of hypotheses which might be examined, discussed, and ultimately tested empirically. Otherwise, the theory of catharsis will remain in limbo; one cannot define the cathartic processes without empirical tests, but one cannot make empirical tests without theoretical definitions, and so on, around in circles.

There is one cathartic therapy which contains explicit definitions of the cathartic processes, namely Reevaluation Counseling (RC). As a basis for a provisional theory of catharsis which can then be subject to test, I will use the RC framework, which defines seven emotional distresses, and their associated cathartic reflexes:

Emotional Distress	Cathartic Process
1. Grief	Crying
2. Intense Fear	Involuntary trembling, cold sweat
3. Moderate Fear, embarrassment	Spontaneous laughter
4. Rage	Storming, with hot sweat
5. Anger	Spontaneous laughter
6. Boredom (stimulus deprivation)	Spontaneous, nonrepetitive talk
7. Physical injury or tension	Yawning, stretching, scratching

(Jackins, 1965; see also Scheff, 1972)

The empirical basis for this list of discharge processes and their associated distresses is observation of clients in therapy. I have observed that among my clients, those who cry, laugh, shiver, and so on, in therapy, make rapid progress, and those who don't, progress slowly or not at all. I assume that Jackins derived the list originally in the same way, by observing the accompaniments of therapeutic change.

This list is intended to be exhaustive of all the processes of emotional discharge, but not exhaustive of all distresses. The distresses named here are simply the most primitive. Many complex emotions may be combinations of two or more of these distresses. Depression, for example, may be a mixture of anger and grief. The naming of complex emotions is complicated by the phenomenon of distancing. I will return to this issue after the discussion of distancing below.

According to this theory, there are four basic distressful emotions: grief, fear, anger, and boredom. These emotions are physical states of tension in the body which are produced by stress. For example, if a stranger slaps your face, there is not only physical but also emotional distress, usually a mixture of grief, fear, and anger. The fact that these emotions are tension states can be most clearly seen in the case of fear. The symptoms of acute fear—pallor, chill in the extremities, and rapid and shallow breathing—are caused by tension: constriction in the blood vessels, which interferes with the circulation of the blood, causing pallor and chill in the hands and feet, and constriction in the bronchi, interfering with oxygen intake, leading to rapid, shallow breathing.

The theory further specifies that, in the absence of interference, these tension states will be spontaneously discharged by convulsive, involuntary bodily processes, whose external manifestations are weeping (for grief), shivering and cold perspiration (for fear), spontaneous laughter (for embarrassment or anger), and "storming" (rapid, forceful movement and vocalization) with hot perspiration, also for anger. This theory provides, therefore, a detailed and explicit definition of catharsis. The dis-

49

charge of the distressful emotions (catharsis) is defined as largely internal, involuntary processes, with invariant external indicators such as weeping, shivering, cold sweating, and so on. For a parallel statement on the relationship between distress and tension, see Plutchik (1954).

Note that the theory makes a sharp distinction between emotion as distress, and emotion as discharge. This distinction is not ordinarily made. We are accustomed to lumping together, for example, the pallor, chill, and panting of the distress of fear with the shivering and cold sweating of the discharge of fear. The theory insists that emotional distress and discharge are two different and, in fact, opposite processes. The signs of emotional distress are symptomatic of increasing muscular and visceral tension, just as the signs of emotional discharge are indicative of the relaxation of tension. Our very language seems at fault, since the nouns which we use to designate emotions lead us to think in terms of states rather than processes, and we do not possess suitable terms to differentiate between the distress of grief, fear, embarrassment, and anger, and their discharge. Perhaps a new set of terms which are all verbs is needed: griefing, fearing, embarrassing, angering, for the distress side of the emotions, and degriefing, defearing, deembarrassing, deangering, for the discharge side.

If there is no interference, the discharge process will continue until the tension is relieved. An infant who is separated from its mother may, when the mother returns, go through all of these processes in rapid succession or even simultaneously—crying, shaking, laughing, and, finally, babbling happily. This is assuming that the mother will allow it. Many mothers, however, are usually not tolerant. The infant may be coerced into stopping. It would seem, in fact, that in modern societies, for most people, there is considerable interference with discharge. Children, especially males, are not allowed to cry, nor are they, especially females, allowed to express all of the anger they feel. Interference by parents ("If you don't stop crying, I'll give you something to cry about"), teacher ("Be a big boy"), and peers ("Cry, baby, cry!") is more or less continuous and systematic. As indicated in Chapter 1, Tomkins (1963, Vol. II, 72–76) argues that the socialization of emotional discharge is usually by punishment rather than reward.

Given the fact that a person can usually expect his emotional expression to be met with punishment, an almost universal strategy is to learn to interfere with one's own discharge: one learns to avoid expressing emotional distress. The boy who is hurt on the playground will hold in his crying until it is safe, in his room. What usually happens, however, is that the techniques of controlling discharge are overlearned—the boy seemingly forgets how to cry, the girl to express anger, except under extreme provocation.

Because of the almost continuous interference with discharge, both by others and by one's own learned reflexes, most individuals accumulate massive amounts of repressed emotion, bodily tension which is always present but usually not recognized. Obviously, the notion that emotions can "accumulate" is only a metaphor, since, as indicated above, emotions are processes. Nevertheless, I will argue here that it is still an extremely useful metaphor. One important consequence of this accumulated emotion is that it serves to transmit to others, and therefore to perpetuate, the repression of emotion in the entire society. The more repressed emotion one has accumulated, the less one can tolerate discharge in others, since it disturbs one's own equilibrium. A mother whose grief is repressed will constantly interfere with her child's crying, producing a child who, in turn, will also accumulate repressed grief, and so on, throughout the generations.

A second consequence of repressed emotion, according to the theory, is the diminution of the clarity of thought and perception. A person in the grip of strong emotion is unable to think clearly and is more or less oblivious to the surrounding environment. (For a study relating distressful emotion and repression, see Lowenfeld, 1961.) This consequence is reflected in such expressions as "I was scared out of my wits," and "I was blind with rage." Unconscious emotion appears to affect thinking and perception in the same way, except that the person is unaware of the cause of the difficulty, as when a woman says, "I don't know why I'm so stupid where men are concerned," or a student, "My mind seems to shut off in algebra."

A third consequence of accumulation of repressed emotion is to interfere with fellow-feeling and cooperativeness and thus to isolate individuals, one from the other. This may be due partly to the negative emotional tone generated by the accumulated emotion itself, feelings of apathy, hollowness, and alienation, and partly by the process of punitive socialization of emotion which produces repression. As Tomkins (1963, Vol. II) explains, the person whose emotions have been socialized punitively has learned to hide his most intense preoccupations from others, since he has found that revelation causes further suffering. Since such a person is unable to share much of his inner life with others, he is apt to be moody and distant. On the other hand, the person whose emotions have been socialized with rewards has learned that his distress need not wall him off from others but can be the "occasion of deepest intimacy and affirmation of love and concern" (p. 106).

According to the theory, when complete discharge occurs these distinctive consequences are avoided. The person becomes more tolerant of discharge in others and thus stops transmitting the pattern of repression. Clarity of thought and perception (in the area of repression) is restored, as well as fellow feeling and cooperativeness. For this reason, collective discharge in a social setting, such as theatre or ritual, has powerful social as well as psychological effects. The feelings of relief from tension, increased clarity of thought and perception, and heightened fellow-feeling which follow collective catharsis give rise to extremely powerful forces of cohesion and group solidarity.

The theory gets its name from the process of reevaluation which is thought to occur when discharge is complete in a particular area of repression. The distressful events which produced the repressed emotion are remembered and reevaluated, in the sense that the aura of malaise is removed. They become events like any other and can be assimilated into one's conscious experience.

Emotion and Context

Implied in the theory is a series of hypotheses connecting each distressful emotion with a certain type of context. It assumes certain inescapable contexts are part of the human condition: attachment and loss, safety and danger, fulfillment and frustration, stimulation and boredom. Attachment to another person or to an object implies the possibility of loss. Obviously there can be no loss without there first being attachment; less obviously, but equally important, it is the possibility of loss which gives meaning and content to attachment.

The fundamental context for grief is loss. Grief would appear to be an inescapable feature of infancy, as a result of intense and incommunicable feelings of separation and loss. Tomkins (1963, Vol. II, 53–55) has suggested that the infant's ability to form objects and attachments to those objects, which are separate from the self, depends in a vital way upon crying.[1] He argues that to the extent the infant is able to cry about a lost object, and therefore work through the loss, to that extent the infant will be able to risk attachment in the future. Conversely, if the infant is unable to resolve the loss, to that extent it will be unwilling to risk attachment. His formulation suggests a process to explain the inability to love that is associated with the masculine role. To the extent that men are socialized not to cry, to that extent their accumulated grief forms a primitive barrier to risking attachment to others.

A similar argument can be made on the prevalence of fear and anger. Fear is generated by danger to life, and anger by frustration. Since the infant is unable to comprehend or control separation, even a brief separation from its mother can generate unbearable waves of grief, fear, or anger. These responses are instinctive and unlearned reactions to separation from adults, who are the infant's only source of nourishment and care.

Embarrassment, generated by loss of face, is ubiquitous during the course of maturation.[2] The most common source of embarrassment is making a mistake in public. Since children must learn most of an entire culture by trial and error, it is virtually impossible to become an adult without having committed innumerable social gaffes. Beginning with toilet training, etiquette of touching one's body, eating, rules of ownership, and respect, the child is

1. The relationship between attachment, loss, and crying is also reviewed in Sadoff (1966) and Bowlby (1969, 1973). For a description of a series of studies linking crying and loss in infants (separation from the mother), see Kagan (1976).

2. A review of descriptions and theories of embarrassment can be found in Sattler (1966). The social bases of embarrassment are explored in Goffman (1956) and Gross and Stone (1964). Lynd (1958) makes a distinction between embarrassment and shame which I will not use here. Rather, I will treat embarrassment, shame, and humiliation as synonymous.

confronted with a seemingly endless obstacle course of norms. Language socialization is particularly significant in this respect, since every child must achieve a very precise command of myriads of rules of meaning, pronunciation, grammar, articulation, and so on. Increasingly as the child interacts with his peers, the slightest mistake in nuance of meaning or fluency may bring ridicule and loss of face. Stuttering and lisping, bloopers and double meanings are the stuff of nightmares of embarrassment.

Apparently, there is also a minimal level of stimulation that human beings need to escape the tension of boredom. This need may be especially strong in infants and young children. Stimulation appears necessary both in a positive sense, for growth and development, as well as in the negative sense of avoiding boredom. There is considerable literature documenting the negative consequences of stimulus deprivation, which is an extreme form of lack of stimulation. (Also, see London, 1972.) At this writing the only evidence available for documenting the contention that nonrepetitive talk signals the discharge of boredom is found in the clinical literature on psychotherapy. The cases in *Studies on Hysteria,* for example, seem to indicate that even sessions which are almost purely verbal may have therapeutic effects.

Finally, the theory makes the conventional assumption that injury or physical tension leads to bodily damage or fatigue, respectively. The theory goes on to suggest that the tension associated with these conditions can be resolved by an internal process of catharsis whose external manifestations are yawning, stretching, and scratching. Apparently the process of yawning is something of a mystery in physiological research (Heusner, 1946).

The connection between context and emotion is summarized here:

	Context		
Associated Emotion or State	*Positive*	*Negative*	*Associated Emotion or State*
Love	Attachment	Loss	Grief
Security	Safety	Severe danger	Fear
Pride	Praise	Loss of face	Embarrassment, shame
Satisfaction	Fulfillment	Severe frustration	Rage
Satisfaction	Fulfillment	Moderate frustration	Anger
Interest	Stimulation	Monotony	Boredom
Contentment	Health, relaxation	Injury, tension	Physical damage, fatigue

Repression, Distancing, and Catharsis

Let us consider four distressful emotions—embarrassment, anger, fear and grief. As indicated above, I am assuming that the emotion of embarrassment arises from loss of face in a social situation, as in making an obvious mistake or error. I will further assume that the emotion itself is at least in part a physiological state involving a specific pattern of changes in muscular and visceral tension levels, which, in turn, result in changes in respiration and circulation of the blood. One clear outward indication of embarrassment is blushing. As we shall see below, these physiological changes may or may not be accompanied by awareness of acute discomfort.[3] Finally, I will assume that the reflex of spontaneous, involuntary laughter signals the exact and virtually instantaneous resolution of the tension of embarrassment. I am suggesting that involuntary laughter stands in relationship to the tension of embarrassment as the orgasm reflex stands to the tension of sexual arousal.

Masters and Johnson have shown that orgasm relieves vasocongestion (swelling of the erectile tissues) and myotonia (muscle tension) almost instantaneously. They have also found that the genitals of women who have undergone sustained sexual arousal without orgasm are still painfully congested and tense six hours afterwards (Mas-

---

3. The issue of whether emotions can be unconscious has given rise to considerable discussion among psychoanalysts, with the majority opinion being that they can. For a representative statement, see Pulver (1971). As I do, analysts would argue that there is always a mental component to emotions, even unconscious emotions, i.e., in the unconscious mind.

ters and Johnson, 1966, 119). I will assume that emotional arousal has similar properties. The tension of embarrassment may be completely resolved through the bodily process whose outward signal is involuntary laughter, or it may be retained, at least in part, for long periods of time or even indefinitely.[4]

Similar formulations can be stated concerning anger, fear, and grief. I will assume that anger arises in situations of frustration. Anger can be considered to be, in part, a specific pattern of changes in muscular and visceral tension, which result in increased pulse and blood pressure, rapid breathing, and flushing of the upper chest, neck, and face.[5] The outward sign of the exact resolution of this pattern of tension is hot sweat, which occasionally, but not always, may be accompanied by "storming" (loud shouting and violent movement) as in a temper tantrum, or, as in the case of embarrassment, involuntary laughter. Unlike embarrassment, which I am assuming to have only one outward sign of resolution (involuntary laughter), anger has two: either hot sweat or involuntary laughter. If this is true, it would mean that much of the laughter that occurs among children watching violence in cartoons and comedies is a signal that repressed anger is being discharged.

Fear can also be described, in part, as a particular, invariant pattern of physiological changes which result in a decrease in the efficacy of oxygen intake and in the peripheral circulation of the blood. The resulting chill and pallor in the extremities, and the rapid, shallow breathing, or panting, are reliable external indicators of intense fear. The reflex which instantaneously resolves the tension of

4. The possibility that emotional tension can be retained indefinitely is closely related to the hypothesis that psychosomatic disease is caused by continuing unresolved emotional tension. See Dunbar (1954) for an overview.

5. The tension of anger has been well described by Gellhorn and Loofbourrow (1963) in terms of a response of the sympathetic nervous system.

fear is signaled by involuntary shivering or trembling and cold sweat.

Finally, grief can be considered to be the emotional reaction to loss. Gellhorn and Loofbourrow (1963) describe the physiology of grief as the opposite of anger: a parasympathetic response of the autonomic nervous system, involving decrease in pulse and blood pressure and all aspects of bodily activity. As will be seen in the next chapter, the relationship of grief to autonomic activation is not clear in the literature. (See Averill, 1968.) Although a casual description of facial changes during the distress of grief might give the impression of general loss of muscle tone, facial tension actually increases. Izard (1971, 242) describes a number of such increases, including what appear to be the two major changes: muscles in the forehead contracted, pulling the eyebrows together, and tension in the mouth and jaw, pulling the corners of the mouth down, with the center of the lower lip pushed forward. The reflex which resolves the tension of grief is signaled by sobbing with tears.

Engle's study (1971) of sudden deaths following psychological stress suggests that emotional tension can reach lethal levels. Of the 170 cases, he found that the majority occurred after loss (53 percent). The next largest group involved danger (34 percent). The remaining cases he divides into two groups, one which he calls "loss of status or self-esteem" (ten cases) and the other "reunion, triumph, or happy ending" (ten cases). In reading the cases he classifies as loss of status or self-esteem, it appears that most involve humiliation, but in several anger seems to be the predominant emotion. Except for the cases involving positive emotions (about 6 percent of the total) all of the cases can be interpreted as involving the same distressful emotions that have been discussed here: grief, fear, anger, and embarrassment. In the cases involving positive emotions, it could be argued that the positive contexts were not sufficiently distanced to avoid the restimulation of the associated negative emotion: i.e., a reunion could restimulate the memory of separation and loss and therefore bring on an overwhelming reaction of grief.

To summarize this discussion: the distresses of embarrassment, anger, fear, or grief are, in part, bodily states of tension, of which the person may be aware or unaware. These tension states can be exactly resolved through catharsis, whose outward signs are involuntary laughter (for embarrassment or anger), hot sweat (also for anger), shivering and cold sweat (for fear), and sobbing with tears (for grief). The next question which the theory seeks to answer concerns the conditions under which these emotions are retained as states of tension (what Freud [1895] called "strangulated affects"), and under what conditions they are discharged.

The process which the theory suggests as the answer to this question is the distancing of the distressful emotions, which will be defined as the extent to which the person's attention is not taken up by the return of repressed emotion from past events. This definition is consonant with the broader use of the term in dramatic criticism, which I will now review. In dramatic criticism, a drama is considered to be underdistanced if it evokes raw emotion in audiences to the point that its members become so drawn into the dramatic action that they forget where they are; they react as if they were participants in, rather than observers of, the drama. Such experiences increase, rather than decrease, tension levels in the audience. In overdistanced drama, the audience is unmoved. Members of the audience are entirely observers of the dramatic action, with no participation at all.

At aesthetic distance, the members of the audience become emotionally involved in the drama, but not to the point where they forget that they are also observers. Aesthetic distance may be defined as the simultaneous and equal experience of being both participant and observer. Part of the person's attention is in the past, absorbed in reliving a distressful experience that has been restimulated by the present context; however, part of the person's attention is also in the present, realizing that there is no real threat. An analogous, but more abstract idea is represented by Greenson (1967, 47) as the "splitting of the ego," between the irrational, experiencing ego, and the rational cooperative ego, of the patient in psychoanalysis. This splitting of attention solves the paradox of repression. Emotions are repressed when they seem so overwhelming as to be unbearable. ("If I allow myself to get angry, I'll kill someone." "If I start to cry, I'll cry forever.") How is one able to bear unbearable pain? The answer suggested here is that distress which seemed unbearable can be relived in a context in which the person knows that the pain can be escaped should it become overwhelming. When the individual's attention is exactly divided between past distress and present safety (i.e., at optimum distance from the repressed emotion), repression is lifted, and catharsis can occur.

In reevaluation theory the condition for discharge is called "the balance of attention." One's attention is evenly divided between one's distress, which is usually connected with past events, on the one hand, and the realization that one is actually safe and in present time, on the other. A common path to a balance of attention between past distress and the safe present occurs in the counseling situation, where the client, while recounting distressful events, is, at the same time, taking the role of the counselor and therefore seeing his own distress from the outside, at the same time that he is feeling it from the inside. When the balance of attention is achieved, the client is both participant in, and observer of, his own distress. Under these conditions, the repressed emotion ceases to be too overwhelming to countenance; the client becomes sufficiently aware of it to feel it and to discharge it.

Deviation from the point of balance usually keeps discharge from occurring or stops discharge if it has started. If most of one's attention is absorbed by the distress, the distressful event is simply relived, as if it were happening again. Just as one was unable to discharge the distressful emotion in the original event, so one is unable to discharge it in the event as relived. On the other hand, if most of one's attention is in the safe present, the repressed emotion is not sufficiently felt, and, again, no discharge occurs. At the balance point, one is both reliving the event, and therefore feeling the emotions associated with it, and at the same time, observing the distressful event from the safety of the present.

The concepts of the balance of attention and optimum distancing seem to be equivalent. Having too much attention in the distressful event corresponds to "underdistancing" in aesthetic terms, and having too little attention in the distressful event corresponds to "overdistancing." Bullough (1912), for example, uses the argument that a work of art may be "overdistanced" or "underdistanced." Brecht argued that alienation in the theatre is a necessary counterweight to engagement. Maynard Mack (1962) has written of the balance of engagement and detachment in Shakespearean drama, and Kenneth Clark, in his discussion of Titian, has suggested that such a balance is the hallmark of all art: " . . . he could maintain that balance between intense participation and absolute detachment which distinguishes art from all other human activity" (quoted in Mack, 1962).

At aesthetic distance, repressed emotion is restimulated, but the result is not overwhelming. Since one is both participant and observer, one is able to experience the repressed feeling and do what one was unable to do originally, i.e., discharge the distress. At aesthetic distance, one is both participant in, and observer of, one's own distress, so that one can go in and out freely.

I have observed children crying in a way that suggests a cycle of participation and observation. The child draws into himself to feel the pain, puts his head down and cries, but frequently looks up at his mother to see if the situation is still safe. While feeling the pain, the child also sees himself through the mother's eyes, as an observer. Although it is by no means completely clear, adults, under the proper conditions, probably speed up this cycle, moving from participant to observer and back in seconds. The phenomenon of crying when happy may be an instance of moving back and forth between safety and pain so fast that the individual is not aware of the movement. The phenomenon of rapid "micromomentary" changes in facial expression suggests a way of testing the hypothesis that aesthetic distance is the rapid alternation of past and present emotions. For a study of micromomentary changes in facial expression, see Haggard and Isaacs (1966).

Implicit in the concept of distancing is the idea that there are two distinct types of consciousness—present-time and past-time. In present-time consciousness, one is attending to the actual surrounding environment. In past-time consciousness, one is not responding to the present environment (although one may think that one is) but compulsively reexperiencing a distressful scene from the past. The past scene may have been triggered by some stimulus in the present environment, but, once begun, the inner experience transforms the present environment, and one reacts as if one were in the past environment again. Paranoia is a familiar case—one reads hostility into smiling faces.

The degree of distance from one's emotion corresponds

to the extent to which one is responding to the present environment. Total overdistancing involves responding only to the nonemotional aspects of the present environment—there is no emotional resonance at all. Total underdistancing means complete immersion in some past scene and complete oblivion to the present. Aesthetic distance involves a balanced experience of a present and a past scene.

The concept of a continuum of distance suggests a way of looking at repression outside of the theatre. Underdistancing is the return of repressed emotion in a situation in which it is not appropriate. One may believe that one is experiencing the present situation, because the content of the experience is transformed by splitting, projection, displacement, and so on. The emotional content, however, is an exact repetition of the repressed experience. Déjà vu, on the other hand, is typically only slightly underdistanced, with the amount of attention in the present only somewhat less than the amount of attention in the repressed experience.

Transference in everyday life may also be viewed as an underdistanced state. Emotions that originated in an earlier relationship are restimulated by a current relationship. Love at first sight is very likely to be a relationship of this type. When a parent persistently calls his or her child by the wrong name, usually the name of another relative, there is usually a strong undertow of repressed and inappropriate emotion directed at the child. Since the memory of the original relationship is repressed, the parent is usually quite unaware that part of his or her attention toward the child is based not on the child, but on someone else.

At the other extreme, overdistancing represents experiences in which selected emotions, both past and present, have been filtered out of awareness. Overdistanced experience is completely cognitive. At extremes of overdistancing, the individual may complain of feeling empty, hollow, or blank, of not knowing what he or she wants or feels. Most overdistancing is not at this extreme, however. In the masculine role, most, but not all, fear and grief have been filtered out of awareness; these emotions are stored as muscular tension and other physiological anomalies. In the feminine role, much anger and embarrassment lie outside of the woman's awareness. The male role can be viewed as a socially induced "retention hysteria," to use Freud's term, in which the affects of fear and grief are retained and the female role as a retention hysteria in which the affects of anger and embarrassment are retained. Under great stress, or under conditions which relax the repressing forces, such as in the theatre or in psychotherapy, these emotions may be felt and discharged.

At aesthetic distance, there is a balance of thought and feeling. There is deep emotional resonance, but also a feeling of control. If a repressed emotion such as grief is restimulated at aesthetic distance, the crying that results is not unpleasant: it is not draining or tiring—the person feels refreshed when it is over. The same is true with fear, anger, and embarrassment.

The concept of a distancing continuum can be used in classifying various complex emotions such as depression, jealousy, and loneliness. As already indicated, depression may be considered as a mixture of overdistanced grief and anger, jealousy, of overdistanced fear, anger, and embarrassment, and, finally, loneliness of overdistanced grief and boredom. In the case of each of these complex emotions, the degree of overdistancing of one component relative to another, e.g., of grief relative to boredom in loneliness, might change the nature of the emotion as it is experienced. For example, one might expect men to experience jealousy differently from women, even though the same basic emotions are involved for both, assuming that anger and embarrassment are usually less repressed in men than in women, and fear usually less repressed in women than in men. If this were the case, then men would experience jealousy as a mixture of anger and embarrassment, as well as the numb or empty feeling that is associated with a repressed emotion, in this case, fear. Women, on the other hand, might experience jealousy as fear and the numb feeling associated with the repression of anger and embarrassment. The exact shading of emotions as they are experienced is far too complex an issue to be examined here in any detail. For this reason, I will limit my analysis to the simple, unalloyed emotions discussed initially.

The characteristics of the various states of emotion when over-distanced, underdistanced, and at aesthetic distance follow:

Emotional States and Distance

Type of Distress	Underdistanced	At Aesthetic Distance	Overdistanced
Grief	Sadness, with or without tears. Headaches, nasal congestion, swelling of eyes. Feelings of hopelessness.	Sobbing with tears.	Emotionlessness and/or distraction in situation of loss.
Fear	Facial pallor, coldness in hands and feet, rapid and shallow breathing. Rapid heart beat. Feelings of fright and immobility.	Shaking with cold sweat.	Emotionlessness and/or distraction in situation of danger.
Embarrassment	Blushing, immobilization, lowering or covering of eyes and face.	Spontaneous laughter.	Emotionlessness and/or distraction in situation of losing face.
Anger	Violence of movement or speech, repetitiveness.	Hot sweat or spontaneous laughter.	Emotionlessness and/or distraction in situation of frustration.
All of the above distresses:			
During discharge or stress	Pain, feeling of loss of control, tension.	Not unpleasant feeling, feeling of control, relaxation.	No feeling, feeling of control, tension.
After discharge or stress	Exhaustion, confusion of thought, withdrawal.	Exhilaration, clarity of thought, outgoingness.	Tension, clarity of thought, outgoingness.

It should be noted that the concept of distancing is applicable both to the stimuli which can give rise to emotional responses and to the responses themselves. Stimuli which are aesthetically distanced are those that are arranged to represent distress and safety equally. A roller coaster, for example, has these elements engineered into its construction, so that the average participant is expected to feel great danger and complete safety simultaneously. As will be shown in Chapter 6, classical drama has a similar construction, so that most members of the audience are simultaneously induced to feel distressful emotion but are also reminded that they are only observers. On the response side, aesthetic distance refers to the actual emotional response of participants. Since the distancing of the stimulus does not automatically lead to distancing of the response, given enormous variations in the personalities, mood, and context of the responders, both sides of the equation must always be investigated. To use comic drama as an example, even with identical performances (as in film) there is considerable variation in the amount of laughter within and between different audiences.

The theory of catharsis proposed here implies a temporal sequence that can be divided, for conceptual purposes, into four phases: (1) an arrangement of stimuli which is optimally distanced, i.e., which contains a balance of distressful and reassuring stimuli; (2) the participant's response, in which there is a balance between involvement in past distress and present safety; (3) catharsis, which is signaled by sobbing with tears, shivering with cold sweat, etc.; and, finally, (4) decrease in tension, increases in mental clarity, and feelings of well-being. In an unpublished study, I have demonstrated a connection between phase 1, the arrangement of the stimuli in the script of a drama, and phase 3, catharsis in theatre audiences, as signaled by audible laughter. The study reported in Chapter 7 shows the connection between phase 3, catharsis, again signaled by laughter in an audience, and phase 4, tension reduction among the members of the audience.

A formal definition of catharsis may be formulated on the basis of this discussion. In this definition, it is necessary to specify two components. First, for the major distresses (grief, fear, anger, and embarrassment) the somatic component is the emotional content, whose outward signs are crying, shivering, laughing, etc. (Nichols and Zax [1977, 8], refer to this component as "somatic-emotional catharsis—the motoric discharge of emotion in expressive sounds and actions such as tears and sobbing of grief, or the trembling and sweating of fear.") The second component concerns distancing: crying, shivering, laughing, etc., are cathartic to the extent that they occur at aesthetic distance, i.e., to the extent that the individual is both participant in, and observer of, his or her own distress. The subjective signs of aesthetic distance are that the individual feels considerable control over his or her crying, etc.: there is little or no feeling of being overwhelmed or being unable to stop. A second objective sign is that the discharge process is not entirely unpleasant. At exactly optimal distance, the process may be completely pleasant. Finally, the consequences of discharge may be used as a sign: the nearer to optimal distancing, the less negative are consequences (tension, headache, eyes red or swollen, fatigue, etc.), and the more positive are consequences (clarity of thought, relaxation, feelings of renewed energy or exhilaration). The outward signs of optimal distance concern the amount of attention the individual has on the environment; he or she shows more or less continual signs of being aware of the immediate surroundings through tears, shivering, etc., by direction of gaze, gestures, and so on.

Note that this definition makes no mention of the recall of events from the past. The process of remembering distressful events is an important feature of Freud and Breuer's definition of catharsis, and also of that of Nichols and Zax. According to Nichols and Zax's definition, catharsis must contain both the somatic-emotional and what they call the cognitive-emotional component: "the recall of forgotten material" (p. 8). I believe that this definition is unnecessarily limiting, in that it refers only to a special circumstance. This circumstance concerns the emotional content: for the distress of boredom, and for this distress only, a certain kind of verbal recall (nonrepetitive talk, which shows new memories and insights) is the outward sign that catharsis is taking place. For this distress only, there is no somatic discharge.

I believe that the source of the confusion is due in part to Freud and Breuer's techniques: they probably unintentionally encouraged this type of discharge, and discouraged somatic discharge. There is also another source of confusion, however. In many cases it would appear that the recall of forgotten events is blocked until the necessary amount of somatic discharge has taken place. As the patient comes to the end of the somatic discharge, brought on by a particular linking object, sometimes over the course of many, many sessions, memories become unblocked. When somatic discharge is complete, an entire series of events may be recollected with surprising vividness and clarity, giving rise to voluminous nonrepetitive talk. However, according to my definition, most catharsis that occurs is not of this type. For example, in most cathartic laughing and crying, the individual is unaware of the unconscious source of the distress, as in the case of the cathartic processes that take place in an audience in the theatre. Most of the members of the audience, most of the time, do not make any connection between the powerful emotional experiences they undergo and events in their own lives. They usually think of their reactions as caused by the events in the drama. This kind of unaware catharsis is therapeutic in that it can be likened to a slow chipping away at unconscious emotional distress. If the amount of cath?,sis in a particular area exceeds the amount of new distress that is being accumulated in that area, the unconscious source of the distress will ultimately be uncovered.

To summarize the argument, catharsis of the major emotional distresses contains two components: an emotional content, which is signaled by physical processes such as crying and laughing, and optimal distancing, which is signaled subjectively by feelings of control, pleasure, and relief and objectively by the discharging individual's appearance of being in contact with his or her immediate environment. For the distress of boredom, and near the end of a somatic discharge process, catharsis is marked by nonrepetitive talk and particularly by the detailed and vivid recall of forgotten events. It is to this aspect of the cathartic process that the discussion will now turn.

Distancing in the Recall of the Past

In their initial formulation of the process of abreaction, Freud and Breuer conceived of *remembering* the originating trauma as a vital part of the process. Symptoms were removed, they said, if: ". . . we had succeeded in bringing clearly to light the *memory* of the event by which it was provoked . . ." (Freud and Breuer, 1895, 40–41). In some passages, it was indicated that a special kind of remembering was involved: "The psychical process which originally took place may be repeated as vividly as possible; it must be brought back to its *status nascendi* . . ." (ibid., 41). In most descriptions of their technique, however, they seem to be content with the formulation of "vivid remembering" as a description of the process necessary for therapy.

Many years later, Freud acknowledged that more than remembering was involved; the patient must *reexperience* the past: ". . . the patient "is obliged to repeat the repressed material as a *contemporary experience* . . . the patient must *reexperience* some portion of his forgotten life . . ." (Freud, 1961, 12–13, my italics).

The phenomenon of reexperiencing the past has been reported frequently by the great writers of world literature: Flaubert, Baudelaire, Hofmannsthal, Valéry, Virginia Woolf, and Proust. In a recent study, Jephcott (1972) refers to such episodes, "involuntary memory," as a type of "privileged moment," or expanded consciousness. A statement by Virginia Woolf can be taken as an example. She refers to the content of the past event (in this case, a return to a childhood scene in St. Ives) that she reexperienced as a "picture":

The strength of these pictures—but sight was always then so much mixed with sound that picture is not the right word—the strength anyhow of these impressions makes me again digress. These moments—in the nursery, on the road to the beach—can still be more real than the present moment.

. . . .

At times I can go back to St. Ives more completely than I can this morning. I can reach a state where I seem to be watching things happen as if I were there (Woolf, 1976, 67).

The most widely known evocation of this process is found in Proust. Much of his writing seems to have been based less on remembering the past (because of the extraordinary detail of his prose, remembering would have been a prodigious feat) than of reexperiencing it, so that he could describe a scene as it was reoccurring (Jephcott, 1972). Proust has described, in fictional form, his first experience of reliving his childhood, when as a young man, he was given tea and *petites madeleines,* the tea and cake of his childhood:

No sooner had the warm liquid, and the crumbs with it, touched my palate than a shudder ran through my whole body, and I stopped, intent upon the extraordinary changes that were taking place. An exquisite pleasure had invaded my senses, but individual, detached, with no suggestion of its origin. And at once the vicissitudes of life had become indifferent to me, its disasters innocuous, its brevity illusory—this new sensation having had on me the effect which love has of filling me with a precious essence; or rather this essence was not in me, it was myself. I had ceased now to feel mediocre, accidental, mortal (Proust, 1928, 62).

At first puzzled by his response, he finally remembers the source:

The taste was that of the little crumb of madeleine which on Sunday mornings at Combray (because on those mornings I did not go out before church-time), when I went to say good-day to her in her bedroom, my aunt Leonie used to give me, dipping it first in her own cup of tea. The sight of the little madeleine had recalled nothing to my mind before I tasted it; perhaps because I had so often seen such things in the interval, without tasting them . . . that their image had dissociated itself from those Combray days to take its place among others more recent; perhaps because of those memories, so long abandoned and put out of mind, nothing now survived, everything was scattered; the forms of things . . . were either obliterated or had been so long dormant as to have lost the power . . . which would have allowed them to resume their place in my consciousness. But when from a long-distant past nothing subsists, after the things are broken and scattered, still, alone, more fragile, but with more vitality, more unsubstantial, more persistent, more faithful, the smell and taste of things remain poised a long time . . . ready to remind us . . . amid the ruins of all the rest; and bear unfaltering, in the tiny and almost impalpable drop of their essence, the vast structure of recollection (ibid., 65).

It's not that he suddenly remembers scenes from his childhood; rather, they reoccur:

. . . once I had recognized the taste of the crumb of madeleine
. . . which my aunt used to give me . . . immediately the old
grey house upon the street, where her room was, rose up like the
scenery of a theatre to attach itself to the little pavilion, opening
on to the garden, which had been built out behind it for my
parents (the isolated panel which until that moment had been all
that I could see); and with the house the town, from morning to
night and in all weathers, the Square where I was sent before
luncheon, the streets along which I used to run errands, the
country roads we took when it was fine. And just as the Japanese
amuse themselves by filling a porcelain bowl with water and
steeping in it little crumbs of paper which until then are without
character or form, but, the moment they become wet, stretch
themselves and bend, take on color and distinctive shape, become flowers or houses or people, permanent and recognizable,
so in that moment all the flowers in our garden and in M.
Swann's park, and the water-lilies on the Vivonne and the good
folk of the village and their little dwellings and the parish church
and the whole of Combray and of its surroundings, taking their
proper shapes and growing solid, sprang into being, town and
gardens alike, from my cup of tea (ibid., 65–66).

The idea that one's total experience may become available for reliving receives support from clinical experience
and from the experiences reported by literary figures such
as Virginia Woolf. It also receives support from a rather
unexpected source, the experiments of a neurosurgeon. In
the course of mapping the regions of the brain through
electrical stimulation, Wilder Penfield found a region in
which the responses seem to fit exactly the model of
aesthetic distance described here: "A young man, J. T.,
who had recently come from . . . South Africa, cried out
when the superior surface of his right temporal lobe was
being stimulated: 'Yes, Doctor! . . . Now I hear people
laughing—my friends in South Africa. . . .' It seemed to
him that he was with his cousins at their home where he
and the two young ladies were laughing together"
(Penfield and Roberts, 1959, 50). In the case of another
patient, A. B.: "(She) heard the singing of a Christmas
song in her church at home in Holland. She seemed to be

there in the church and was moved again by the beauty of the occasion, just as she had been on that Christmas Eve some years before'' (ibid., 52). After describing a large number of similar cases, Penfield says: ''The experiential responses of the flashback variety were, for the most part, quite unimportant moments in the patient's life; standing on a street corner, hearing a mother call her child, taking part in a conversation, listening to a little boy as he played in the yard. If these unimportant minutes of time were preserved in the ganglionic records . . . why should it be thought that any experience in the stream of consciousness drops out . . . ?'' (ibid., 53). Penfield's evidence suggests that the totality of experience is permanently recorded, available at all times during the person's life, as required by the present theory.

Moreover, Penfield makes a second point which is important for this paper. Returning to the case of J. T., he says:

After stimulation was over, he could discuss his double awareness and express his astonishment, for it had seemed to him that he was with his cousins at their home where he and the two young ladies were laughing together . . .
It is significant, however, that during the re-creation of that past experience he was not impelled to speak to his cousins. Instead, he spoke to the ''Doctor'' in the operating room. Herein may lie an important distinction between this form of hallucination and the hallucination of a patient during . . . a psychotic state (ibid., 50, 51).

The distinction that Penfield makes between the ''flashbacks'' of his patients and the psychotic hallucinations exactly corresponds to the difference between what I have called experience at aesthetic distance, which is a precise balance between past and present experience, and completely underdistanced experience, the total return of an overwhelming emotional state from the past. Penfield was able to produce these flashbacks in some of his patients, without fail, by stimulating the proper area of the brain, which he refers to as the interpretive cortex. Furthermore, in virtually every case, the flashbacks appeared to be made up of the equal copresence of past and present (ibid., 51). Finally, he notes, in passing, that the flashbacks are sometimes accompanied by feelings or expressions of emotion, for example, fear (Penfield and Roberts, 1959; Mullen and Penfield, 1959; Penfield and Perot, 1963).

We are now in a position to assess the effectiveness of Freud and Breuer's techniques, from the point of view of the theory of catharsis stated above. Given our discussion of catharsis, this assessment should be made along three major dimensions: the emphasis upon verbal as opposed to nonverbal processes, memory versus reoccurrence, and repetition as opposed to singular occurrences in therapy. First of all, it would seem that Freud and Breuer emphasized the verbal content of therapy, as against the nonverbal, emotional processes. They repeatedly refer to their approach as "the talking cure." In their definition of catharsis, they give a prominent place to verbally expressed recollection of traumatic events: ". . . when the patient has *described* that event in the greatest possible detail and put the *affect* into *words*" (Freud and Breuer, 1895, 41). They also acknowledge the importance of emotion: "[the curative process involves] . . . bringing clearly to light the memory of [the trauma] . . . and in arousing its accompanying affect . . ." (ibid., 41). However, in their actual case descriptions, it is clear that by "arousal of affect" they are usually referring to a very low level of emotional arousal (e.g., animated talk). Although the processes which may have signaled emotional discharge in the sense discussed above are occasionally mentioned (e.g., crying), in the main, Freud and Breuer made little of the distinction I am suggesting as crucial: the distinction between emotional discharge as signaled by crying, shivering, sweating, or laughing, and all other emotional reactions.

The second dimension involves the difference between remembering and reexperiencing. Again, it is clear that in some episodes, the patients were reexperiencing past events, rather than merely remembering them—the cases of Cäcilie and Elizabeth are particularly rich in this regard, and in other cases, like that of Anna O., there are single instances of the reoccurrence of a trauma which are given focal importance. In the main, however, Freud and Breuer are quite accepting of verbal memories, rather than highly emotional reoccurrences, as the basic events that are necessary for cathartic therapy. If the patient spontaneously experienced the reoccurrence of a trauma, it was accepted as part of the therapy, but Freud and Breuer did not usually seek reexperiencing as a routine part of therapy.

The last dimension involves the question of repetition. In the case of the highly gifted lady, Freud himself raised this question, as already indicated above: was she repeatedly abreacting the same scene, or rather was she responding to different details each time? Freud and Breuer's theory suggested the latter interpretation, since they believed it necessary that the patient progress through her file, abreacting to each trauma and symptom occurrence once. This case, and others involving the abreaction of arrears, are susceptible to a quite different interpretation, however. That is, what is necessary is a repeated discharge of emotional tension with which exactly the same scene is charged. Let us examine another of Freud's cases, Mathilde H.:

I once learnt to my surprise that an "abreaction of arrears" . . . can form the subject-matter of an otherwise puzzling neurosis. This was so in the case of Fräulein Mathilde H., a . . . nineteen-year-old girl. When I first saw her she was suffering from a partial paralysis of the legs. Some months later, however, she came to me for treatment on account of a change in her character. She had become depressed . . . , utterly inconsiderate to her mother, irritable and inaccessible. . . . She was very easily put into a state of deep somnambulism, and I [gave] her commands and suggestions at every visit. She listened to these in deep sleep, to the accompaniment of floods of tears. . . . One day . . . she told me that the cause of her depression was the breaking off of her engagement. . . . Closer acquaintance with her fiancé had brought out . . . things that were unwelcome to her and her mother. . . . For a long time they had both wavered. . . . In the end her mother uttered the decisive negative on her behalf. A little later she had woken up as though from a dream and begun to occupy her thoughts busily with the decision that had already been made. . . . This process, she told me, was still going on. . . . I did not succeed in inducing the girl to talk again. I continued to address her while she was in deep somnambulism and saw her burst into tears each time without ever answering me; and one day, round about the anniversary of her engagement, her whole state of depression passed off—an event which brought me the credit of a great therapeutic success by hypnotism (Freud and Breuer, 1895, 204–205).

Although the patient was cured, she was relegated to a footnote. She didn't satisfy Freud's preconceived theory: he thought that the trauma and its accompanying affect had to be described in words, and Mathilde H. cried her depression away. Freud found her case surprising and puzzling, but, conscientious observer that he was, he reported it anyway.

The case of Mathilde H. and the highly gifted lady seem to me to be critical for evaluating the difference between Freud and Breuer's theory and the revised theory that is offered here. The therapeutic technique in the two cases is unambiguously successful: Mathilde H. was completely cured, and the highly gifted lady never developed symptoms. Yet their cases do not fit Freud and Breuer's theory and technique: there was virtually no verbal recounting of a series of traumatic events. Instead, cure was achieved through a highly repetitive reenactment of past scenes, with profuse weeping.

The cases of Mathilde H. and the highly gifted lady suggest the necessity for modifying Freud and Breuer's technique in two substantial ways. First, they suggest that for the repressed affects of grief, fear, and anger, which constitute the major emotional distresses, that verbal recollection stands in relation to the cathartic process only as a means to an end. Verbal recall can serve as a means of restimulating the exact emotional components of a traumatic scene or scenes. But for the major affects, verbal recall is neither necessary nor sufficient for catharsis. It is not necessary since there are also other devices which can give rise to restimulation. Sensory stimuli, such as Proust's experience with tea and a madeleine, have already been discussed; music, dance, and drama have a similar direct emotional impact on occasion. In "regrief" therapy for pathological bereavement, mementos which serve as reminders of the loss are used. These mementos are called "linking objects"; they may be photographs, clothing, or other keepsakes which evoke reoccurrence of repressed emotions connected with bereavement (Volkan, 1975).

Neither is verbal recall sufficient in itself for therapy, except for the one affect of boredom. Freud and Breuer explicitly pointed out that recall without affect was ineffective. The cases of Mathilde and the highly gifted lady make the corollary point: emotional discharge without verbal recall *is* effective. The highly gifted lady wept repeatedly over the same losses with very little verbal recall and Mathilde H. had virtually none. In summary, this discussion suggests that, for the major repressed affects, verbal recall is neither necessary nor sufficient for therapy, and emotional discharge is both necessary and sufficient.

The cases of Mathilde H. and the highly gifted lady

suggest a second point, a point about the need for repeated experiences of abreaction. Unlike Anna O., Mathilde's and the highly gifted lady's therapy apparently did not require them to reexperience their whole file of traumas and the occurrence of symptoms. In these two cases, the cathartic process appeared to require repeatedly weeping over the same critical scene or, possibly, as Freud suggests, over different details of the same scene. At the time of this writing, there doesn't appear to be any empirical basis for choosing between the two ideas: exact repetition, scene by scene, until every scene in the file is exhausted, on the one hand, or repeated reexperiencing of the same scene, but each repetition emphasizing a different detail. In his latter writing, Freud appeared to have selected the first possibility: "Thus it was necessary to reproduce the whole chain of pathogenic memories in chronological order, or rather in reversed order, the latest ones first and the earliest ones last, and it was quite impossible to jump over the later traumas in order to get back more quickly to the first, which was often the most potent one" (Freud, 1910, 14). Note that Freud suggests that the first trauma in the file was often the most potent. This thought is made primary in Primal Therapy, which seeks repeated reenactment of the earliest distressful scene.

The distancing paradigm suggests a third alternative. According to this paradigm, verbal recall is ineffective because it is overdistanced; the patient is too much an observer, and not enough of a participant in the emotional distress connected with the past scene. At the other end of the continuum, exact reoccurrence of the trauma is also ruled out. Exact reoccurrence would be underdistanced; the patient would be too much of a participant, and not enough of an observer, to allow discharge to take place. What is required is the distanced reoccurrence of the trauma: at optimal distance, the patient is equally participant and observer. The discovery that many of Freud and Breuer's patients possessed a file of traumatic events may be interpreted as supporting what Tomkins has called a "snowball model" (1963, II, 80–81), for the development of neurotic symptoms. Just as a snowball increases in size going down a hill, so a neurotic pattern leads to situations which produce more distress, which is in turn repressed so that the neurotic pattern is further reinforced. Anna O.'s symptom of being unable to hear originated because of an accidental association between not hearing and the occurrence of extreme distress. To the extent that this symptom, in later situations, led to distressful emotions which were also repressed, a file of traumas was created. After the discussions of drama, games, and ritual in later chapters, I will return to the question of the need for repeated discharge of the emotions in the same or similar scenes in the file.

Conclusion

Freud and Breuer's technique of cathartic therapy has been evaluated in the light of a new and explicit theory of catharsis. This evaluation suggests that their technique was critically flawed: they believed that a single verbal description of a memory of a trauma constitued a sufficient abreaction. From the point of view of the new theory, such a technique would usually be insufficient, discharging only one component, boredom, if that. What is needed is a repeated emotional discharge of fear, grief, anger, and so on, during a properly distanced reexperiencing of a traumatic scene. I have argued that it was Freud and Breuer's failure to follow such a procedure, rather than the lack of validity of cathartic therapy, which would account for most of the difficulties they encountered with their use of catharsis. I will now turn to the issue of the scientific status of the theory of catharsis.

4.

Scientific Theories of Emotion and the Evidence

In all the vast scientific and clinical literature on emotions, there are very few studies which have direct bearing on the theory of catharsis offered here. In the majority of studies, the issue of catharsis simply doesn't arise; most of the literature is concerned with emotional arousal or expression or with static descriptions of various discrete emotional states: joy, fear, anxiety, shame, anger, grief, and so on. No distinction is made between emotion as distress and as discharge. Even a sophisticated commentator like Tomkins fails to make this distinction. His brilliant discussion of the dynamics of grief is confusing for this reason (Tomkins, 1963, II, 47–117).

There is a large body of commentary and study that does concern catharsis, but its relevance to the present theory is also limited. The term catharsis is used in so many different ways, with so wide a variety of definitions, or, in many cases, with no definitions at all (as indicated in the last chapter), that clear evidence for or against the theory is difficult to come by. There is an enormous clinical literature which could be cited, but its implications are ambiguous, not only because catharsis is usually not defined in any clear way, but because of ambiguities in the reporting of case material.

One of the sources of ambiguity is the polemical nature of some of the reports. Partisans, like Janov, or anticatharsis clinicians, like Binstock (1973), may be biased in the cases they choose and in the details they give. Even when there is no explicit ideological stance, the conceptual frame in which case material is reported makes it difficult to make definite inferences about the effects of catharsis. To illustrate this difficulty, I will review several articles concerning the relationship between crying and illness.

Some writers take an unequivocal positive stance but do not give sufficient detail to allow the reader to judge the validity of the writer's interpretation. For example, Foxe (1941) states: "I have observed that many forms of illness show a tendency to recover after weeping or crying," but presents no case material at all. At the opposite extreme, many clinicians see crying or weeping as part of the illness. Heilbrunn (1955), for example, describes the case of a thirty-four-year-old unmarried student of psychology in this way:

Soon after beginning analysis weeping became the outstanding symptom during analytic hours and at other times. Often she fought against her tears, but invariably they would well up, soak many handkerchiefs, and drop on the pillow, her dress, and the couch, until she was veritably bathed in tears. The weeping became almost constant in two out of three analytic sessions, varying in intensity from a furtive tear to uninterrupted sobbing lasting for several minutes and punctuating the hour with paroxysms. She and I were puzzled because the tears were so often inappropriate to what she was saying. She would weep whether she reported a dream, recalled scenes from her childhood, or talked about daily events. Sometimes she would laugh through her tears when their incongruity was so marked as to approach the comic. Usually she consoled herself—and perhaps also me—by saying that she never had dared to cry in the presence of her previous analyst and that this release must be a sign of progress. Eventually it became clear that she responded tearfully not only to her own communications but also with increasing frequency to my interpretations: she explained that it was not the specific interpretation that moved her but rather the resulting overwhelming gratification of being understood or, more often, the feeling of being misunderstood. The pain from being misunderstood could be unequivocally traced to an actual or fantasied attitude of her parents toward her (246).

After narrating the course of treatment, Heilbrunn describes the end of treatment: "Fantasies about her father's expected death and her mother's ensuing emotional collapse led to the disclosure of real and imagined childhood occurrences [which Heilbrunn goes on to describe], which not only explained her attack on me but also solved her principal problem and ended her weeping" (249). The writer has conceptualized the crying as part of the illness; the cure is a result of what she conceives to be the treatment, i.e., the revelation of memories of childhood traumas. In her view when the patient is cured, her symptoms, including crying, stop.

However, there is nothing in the material furnished in the article to preclude a different interpretation, in which the crying was part of the therapeutic process. In this view the crying and the remembering of childhood would be reciprocally related—the crying led to the memories, the memories to further crying, and so on. Unfortunately, there seems to be no objective way of deciding between these two conflicting interpretations.

Even in articles which explicitly posit a link between cure and crying, the writers often stop short of asserting that crying causes the cure. Grinker, like many other clinicians, has noted that depressives do not weep. He goes on to say, "depressed patients begin to recover as they become able to weep" (Grinker, 1953, 137). This passage occurs in the context of a discussion of the amount of fluids in the body. (He sees depressives as dry, psychosomatic patients as wet.) It does not occur in the context of a discussion of catharsis. It would probably never occur to Grinker to see the crying as the curative agent. He might see crying as merely associated with some other curative process.

A similar stance can be found in reports on the link between crying and two psychosomatic illnesses: asthma and hives. French (1939) has observed that many asthma attacks end when crying begins. One study of asthma posits direct connection between catharsis and relief of symptoms. Doust and Leigh (1953) interviewed thirty asthma patients. In the course of the interviews, many of these patients produced what Doust and Leigh called ''the motor expression of emotion, i.e., weeping, laughing, the acting out of anger . . .'' (p. 304), which proved to reduce symptoms and remove the oxygen deprivation which characterized these patients. Unlike the other clinicians cited here, Doust and Leigh see the ''motor expression of emotion'' as the curative agent. Weiner (1977, 252) notes that in addition to French and Doust and Leigh, there are three other reports that ''once the suppressed cry was expressed, the asthma attack ceased.'' He also cites one study, by Knapp and Nemetz (1957) which failed to confirm this hypothesis.

Less direct but suggestive data on the relationship between emotional expression and asthma has been reported by Dirks et al. (1978). They developed a scale of the expression of panic and fear which they gave to asthmatics on first treatment. They found hospitalization for asthma attacks was twice as high for patients who scored either high or low on the Panic-Fear Scale. They interpret this finding to mean that both exaggeration and denial of symptoms are equally maladaptive for asthmatics. This interpretation is congruent with the theory of distancing of emotions offered in this book: both underdistanced and overdistanced emotions are likely to lead to further attacks.

In describing a case of a woman with hives (urticaria) Saul and Bernstein (1941) state: "When she wept she did not have urticaria and the attacks usually terminated with weeping. Conversely, when she repressed her weeping she developed urticaria." Similar findings are reported by Seitz (1951) and by Graham and Wolf (1950). I would be willing to interpret the link between crying and cure in depression, asthma, and hives as support for the theory of catharsis, but none of the reports do so (except for Doust and Leigh).

Another problem with this literature is its scattered nature. Processes of catharsis are described in a wide variety of disciplines: not only in psychiatry and psychology, but in anthropology, physiology, the history of religion, psychosomatic medicine, and many other fields. In each of these bodies of literature, crying and the other cathartic processes are usually mentioned in passing. They are treated as an incidental aspect of the phenomena being discussed and are seldom indexed. In order to find these passages, one has to have read the entire text.

The Nichols and Zax Study

Fortunately for our purposes, a recent study presents a clear review of much of the relevant literature, using a concept of catharsis which seems to be quite similar to the one used in this book. I refer to the study by Nichols and Zax (1977), in which evidence concerning catharsis is reviewed in the following fields: religious and magic healing rites, psychoanalysis, clinical hypnotherapy and the treatment of the traumatic neuroses of war, group therapy, bereavement, behavior therapy, and the social psychology of aggression. In this section, I will begin by discussing the concept of catharsis used by Nichols and Zax. I will then summarize their findings in the various fields they review. Finally, I will review some relevant studies which they missed and give my own assessment of the state of evidence with respect to the catharsis hypothesis. Nowhere do Nichols and Zax offer a formal definition of catharsis, but, if one combines some of their separate statements, one sees that their concept of catharsis is similar to the one I am using. Their clearest statement is as follows:

. . . catharsis has two related but separate components: one is relatively intellectual—the recall of forgotten material; the second is physical—the discharge of emotion in tears, laughter, or angry yelling. The cognitive-emotional aspect consists of the contents of consciousness during the reexperiencing of an emotional event. The somatic-emotional aspect consists of the motoric discharge of emotion in expressive sounds and actions such as the tears and sobbing of grief, or the trembling and sweating of fear (Nichols and Zax, 1977, 8).

They take a position like mine, that both the cognitive-emotional aspect and the somatic-emotional aspect are necessary components of the cathartic process. Note that the examples of the physical process of discharge that they give—tears, laughter, angry yelling, and, in the last part of the statement, the trembling and sweating of fear—subsume the major emotions proposed in the theory of emotions described in this book: grief, fear, embarrassment, and anger.

Nichols and Zax first complain of the amount of bias concerning catharsis in the literature they review—both positive and negative bias: "Those who favor catharsis in therapy describe its effects in pleasant figurative language, while those who do not opt for hyperbolic and fatuous images. This semantic confusion, of course, impedes our understanding of catharsis. So, too, does the virtual absence of empirical research.'' They do find considerable evidence supporting cathartic theory, however.

With respect to religious and magic healing rites, they conclude: '' . . . we found catharsis, along with suggestion, to be of major importance. . . . although no acceptable scientific proof exists that the sort of rituals we reviewed are successful in changing behavior, it seems probable, considering their longevity, that they accomplished some changes. The ubiquity of catharsis in these ceremonies suggests that it is a basic mechanism of behavior change. There is an undeniable vitality in any procedure which has been extant for so long.'' My own survey of the literature on curing rites produced evidence on this point additional to theirs, which may be found on pp. 121–24 in this book.

They come to a similar conclusion concerning hypnotherapy:

. . . we can conclude that hypnotism helps to potentiate catharsis by relaxing the usual prohibitions against emotional discharge—particularly when combined with the suggestion that emotional discharge will follow.

It seems that catharsis is a reasonably natural occurrence when people are given "permission" to experience their feelings, but that powerful techniques, such as hypnotism, are often required to overcome defenses against emotional expression.

In reviewing studies of the effectiveness of catharsis in psychotherapy, Nichols and Zax find only one study which tests the catharsis hypothesis directly, a study conducted by Nichols (1974) himself. In a group of forty-three patients, he assigned emotive therapy to every second patient, and nonemotive (insight-oriented) therapy to every other patient. Furthermore, in his analysis, he takes the step necessary to test the effect of catharsis itself: he partitions the patients in terms of the amount of catharsis they experienced. Comparing the third of the patients with the highest amount of discharge with the third with the lowest, he tests the hypothesis that it is catharsis which leads to therapeutic improvement. His evidence supports his hypothesis on most, but not all, of the measures of improvement used in the study. Nichols and Zax summarize as follows:

Nichols' study demonstrated that the techniques of cathartic therapy produce dramatically high levels of somatic-emotional catharsis. This finding is far from trivial, because it demonstrates the extreme difference between this type of treatment and traditional forms of talking therapy in producing prolonged and intense emotional discharge. Even sessions described by therapists as being highly emotional rarely contain more than five minutes of crying. The use of cathartic techniques, on the other hand, produced sessions in which twenty minutes of profound crying was typical.
Furthermore, emotive patients showed greater improvement on some measures, and this superiority was even more pronounced when those who showed highest levels of discharge were compared with those who showed least discharge.

They fail to mention a second study which seeks to test the effect of catharsis, conducted by Karle et al. (1973). In a study of patients in Primal Therapy, Karle and his coworkers have shown that there is a significant decrease in indicators of bodily tension levels, such as pulse, blood pressure, temperature, etc. Since this study does not show that these changes are caused by the discharge of emotional distress, rather than some other feature of the therapy, it does not provide much direct support for the catharsis hypothesis.

Nichols and Zax also review evidence provided by studies of the effects of therapies ordinarily not regarded as cathartic: implosive and behavioral therapies, client-centered therapies, analogue studies, and the treatment of psychosomatic disorders (159–186). They suggest that these studies provide partial support for the theory of catharsis, since all of the methods seem to lead to high levels of emotional expression, which may, in part, be cathartic and which lead to improvement.

Nichols and Zax also review the social-psychological studies of aggression and come to the same conclusion as I have, that these studies have little relevance to the theory of catharsis: '' . . . this research is not directly relevant to cathartic psychotherapy, because indulging in or observing aggressive behavior is quite different from encouraging cognitive- and somatic-emotional discharge of previous distressful experiences.'' My own view is very similar: the studies of ''aggression catharsis'' in small group laboratories use aggressive *behavior,* rather than emotional discharge, as the treatment variable, which limits their relevance to the theory outlined here. In this same tradition of research, even the studies of ''vicarious aggression,'' which would seem more relevant to my thesis, do not measure the amount and kind of emotional discharge. They use exposure to a stimulus of vicarious aggression as the independent variable. These studies, like the studies of aggressive behavior, could be made relevant to the catharsis hypothesis if they included a measurement of emotional discharge. Until such studies are conducted, the large body of literature on aggression catharsis cannot be used to evaluate the theory proposed here.

They also review ''analogue'' studies of neurotic process (172–181) and studies of attitude change produced by catharsis (191–194). In both kinds of studies, they find evidence at least partially supporting the theory of catharsis. The most impressive section of the Nichols and Zax review is found in their chapter on bereavement (Chapter 6, pp. 80–103). They describe some twenty-five original studies, in which the relationship between grieving and catharsis is demonstrated in a way that supports the theory of catharsis. They state that these studies:

underscore the point that catharsis is particularly relevant in cases of recent emotional distress. We also found the widest agreement among experts of the importance of experiencing and expressing the painful feelings accompanying the death of someone who was close. Most religious traditions and virtually all mental health experts encourage emotional catharsis during bereavement. Certainly, therapists should help their patients to grieve for a lost family member or friend. Furthermore, the logical extension of this wisdom is that catharsis is a helpful way to resolve any loss. Other losses less dramatic, such as the death of a cat or dog, or less tangible, such as the awareness of growing old, probably require catharsis for optimum resolution.

Although Nichols and Zax spent six years reviewing some 294 studies for their relevance to the theory of catharsis, it should not be thought that they are uncritically accepting of catharsis as a therapeutic procedure. In their summary of implications for therapeutic practice, they spend some twenty-five pages in pointing out limitations of cathartic theory and practice. They are especially critical of the notion of the storage of emotional distress and of other conceptions associated with many cathartic therapies, e.g., that all patients should get cathartic therapy, that catharsis alone is sufficient therapy, and that patients should be encouraged to practice catharsis as fully outside of therapy as inside.

In the main, however, the evidence that Nichols and Zax review persuade them that the theory of catharsis is sufficiently valid that it at least warrants further detailed investigation. One incident they note in their historical account is worthy of further mention here, since it is also indicative of present-day attitudes toward catharsis. At the height of his popularity as a healer in the eighteenth century, the hypnotist Anton Mesmer was investigated by a Royal Commission of eminent scientists. The results of the investigation were negative, which had the effect of a condemnation from the then-current Academy of Science. The commission, however, did not investigate the effectiveness of Mesmer's practices but only the accuracy of his theoretical explanations. Since these explanations (which were in terms of magnetic excitation) were easily disproved, Mesmer was condemned: "The Commission . . . did not investigate the . . . (actual) practices, and they failed to note the major role played by emotional excitation and discharge in producing symptom resolution" (Nichols and Zax, 1977, 45). A similar attitude is still found today in many scientific discussions of catharsis: there is a clear negative bias in assessing the evidence that is available.

The bias against catharsis is noted in passing by Yalom, whose work on group psychotherapy is widely known. Speaking of catharsis, he says: "This low prestige but irrepressible curative factor appears to operate in virtually every form of psychological healing endeavor," (quoted in Nichols and Zax, p. 71). Since catharsis is almost always mentioned on lists of curative factors (for example, Rosenzweig [1936] suggests that catharsis and the therapist's personality may be the unrecognized critical factors in all forms of psychotherapy), one wonders if there is not systematic bias in those approaches which omit it completely.

The Nature of Emotions:
The Central-Peripheral Controversy

An important issue which is related, albeit indirectly, to the controversy over catharsis concerns the nature of emotions, whether they are central to the body (in the innate biological core of the body) or peripheral (at the outer edges) where they are conditioned. Writers who dismiss catharsis usually assume a peripheralist position. Learning theorists, for example, usually assume that emotions are conditioned and that substitutes for emotions can be conditioned which are completely equivalent.

The centralist theory of emotion is based on an approach suggested by William James: bodily changes directly follow the perception of an exciting fact; "our feeling of the same changes as they occur *is* the emotion" (James, 1892, 375). James suggests that massive changes occur in the viscera and large muscles of the body as a response to stimuli which signal danger, loss, etc. In James' approach, the emotion *is* our awareness of these changes.

My approach is close to James', except that I take his definition, with its physiological emphasis, a step further: emotions are specific patterns of bodily changes, whether or not there is conscious awareness. This step is necessary if one is to speak of unconscious emotions. Bodily changes associated with repressed anger are observable, not by the person experiencing them, but by others. I am postulating a discrete set of physiological changes for each emotion.

James' approach has been severely criticized by the peripheralists, whose argument, in its most extreme form, is that there are no discrete bodily changes for each emotion. Rather, there is one bodily change, arousal, which is modulated by events that take place on the periphery of the body, in the face, in mind, and the environment, which result in the different emotions of fear, anger, etc.

The classic criticism of the centralist position comes from the physiologist W. B. Cannon (1931). He was skeptical for five reasons:

(1) that total separation of the viscera from the central nervous system (by severing the sympathetic connections) does not alter emotional behavior and thus that emotions can be experienced in the absence of visceral stimulation; (2) that the same visceral states appear in many different emotions; therefore the emotion cannot depend solely on a discrete physiological state; (3) that individuals are relatively insensitive to the state of the viscera, so

that it is unlikely that visceral cues could totally account for emotions; (4) that visceral changes seem to be too slow to be the source of emotions; and (5) most important, that artificial induction of visceral change does not produce real emotions.

Tomkins (1963) has emphasized the importance of facial expression in the process of proprioceptive feedback, which may, he argues, result in a differential interpretation of a single central arousal state into different discrete emotions. Lazarus (1966) has proposed a mental process, which he calls *appraisal*, which may be either conscious or unconscious, that may serve the differentiating function.

Although a substantial number of investigations have sought to clarify this controversy, the results are still quite inconclusive. Different investigators have come to different conclusions. Ax (1953) and, independently, Funkenstein (1956) have apparently shown that fear and anger may be differentiated in terms of certain hormonal substances. Fear is associated with increases in epinephrine (adrenalin: a stimulant) levels in the body, and anger with norepinephrine (a vasoconstrictor). On the other hand, Selye (1956) and Persky et al. (1958) have conducted studies which seem to show basic physiological similarities in different emotional states.

An important study, which is usually interpreted as providing strong support for the peripheral position, was conducted by Schachter and Singer (1967). They studied the interaction between physiological changes, information, and social environment. They injected some subjects with epinephrine and others with an inert substance. Some subjects were informed what kinds of reactions they should expect from the drug, others were uninformed, and others were misinformed. The final variable was the social environment: subjects were placed with another person, who they thought had received the same treatment they (the subject) had. Actually the other person was a confederate of the researcher's, who displayed happy behavior in half of the cases and angry behavior in the other. If the centralist position were correct, the information and social environment conditions should have little effect on the emotions felt by the subjects: only the injection of epinephrine or placebo should matter. If the peripheral approach were correct, the subjective feelings of the subjects should be strongly influenced by the two peripheral variables, information and social environment.

Their findings actually provide support for both sides of the controversy. The subjects' evaluations of their emotional states were influenced both by the central and peripheral variables. Since, however, it was found that under certain informational conditions (misinformed subjects) there was a correlation between social environment and subjective emotion (subjects purportedly reported feeling more happy with a happy confederate, more angry with an angry confederate), the study is usually interpreted as decisively supporting the peripheralist argument.

A close reading of Schachter and Singer's design and results, however, gives only weak support for this interpretation. After the exposure to the happy social environment, the subjects' mean response to the question "How good or happy would you say you feel?" is reported on a scale from zero (I don't feel at all happy) to four (I feel extremely happy). Response to a parallel question, on a scale of zero to four, "How irritated, angry, or annoyed would you say you feel at present?" is also reported for the subjects who were exposed to the angry social environment.

A Self-Report Scale is constructed by subtracting a subject's anger score from his happiness score. This scale could thus conceivably be used to compare the effects of social environment on subjective evaluation of emotion,

93

Theory

because it is made up of both the happiness and the anger ratings. Since the anger score was subtracted from the happiness score, the Scale should be interpreted as indicating more happiness (and less anger) the higher the score. The self-report results reported by Schachter and Singer (1967, Tables 2 and 4) are shown in the accompanying tables.

Self-Report of Emotional State in the Euphoria Conditions

Condition	N	Self-report scales	Comparison	p
Epi Inf	25	0.98	Epi Inf vs. Epi Mis	.01
Epi Ign	25	1.78	Epi Inf vs. Epi Ign	.02
Epi Mis	26	1.90	Placebo vs. Epi Mis,	
Placebo	26	1.61	Ign, or Inf	ns

Self-Report of Emotional State in the Anger Conditions

Condition	N	Self-report scales	Comparison	p
Epi Inf	22	1.91	Epi Inf vs. Epi Ign	.08
Epi Ign	23	1.39	Placebo vs. Epi Ign	
Placebo	23	1.63	or Inf	ns

Schachter and Singer also constructed scales based on the confederates' ratings of the subjects' behavior. For the happy condition, they used a scale indicating the extent to which the subject joined the confederate in his euphoric routine: hula-hooping, shooting with a slingshot, throwing paper airplanes or paper basketballs, and so on. The scale is complex in that it depends on the length of time the subjects join the confederate and the wildness of their behavior. Unfortunately, the study does not report the details of the scale construction to the point where the reader can evaluate the meaning of the "Activity Index." We only know from the table that the range of the mean is from 12.72 to 22.56 (see the accompanying table).

Behavioral Indications of Emotional State
in the Euphoria Conditions

Condition	N	Activity index	Mean number of acts initiated
Epi Inf	25	12.72	.20
Epi Ign	25	18.28	.56
Epi Mis	25	22.56	.84
Placebo	26	16.00	.54

p Value		
Comparison	Activity index	Initiates
Epi Inf vs. Epi Mis	.05	.03
Epi Inf vs. Epi Ign	ns	.08
Placebo vs. Epi Mis, Ign, or Inf	ns	ns

For the anger condition, the rating of "Anger Units" was based on the confederate's observations of the extent to which the subject indicated agreement with his (the confederate's) irritated or angry remarks about the questionnaire they were filling out. Agreement was coded as $+2$, disagreement, -2, no response, zero. The range of the mean, as indicated in the accompanying table, is from $-.18$, indicating lack of anger, to $+2.28$, indicating slightly more than one unit mean agreement with an angry remark by the confederate.

Behavioral Indications of Emotional State
in the Anger Conditions

Condition	N	Neutral units	Anger units
Epi Inf	22	+0.07	−0.18
Epi Ign	23	+0.30	+2.28
Placebo	22	−0.09	+0.79

Comparison for anger units	p
Epi Inf vs. Epi Ign	.01
Epi Ign vs. Placebo	.05
Placebo vs. Epi Inf	ns

The first thing that should be noted in the results concerns the magnitude of the effects caused by the experimental manipulations. Although most of these effects are statistically significant, in the sense that it is improbable that the differences could be due to sampling error, their absolute magnitude is small to the point of having only slight significance in a substantive sense. For the self-report of happiness, the range of the mean is from .98 (1.0 means "I feel a little happy and good") to 1.9 (2.0 means "I feel quite happy and good," 3.0 "I feel very happy and good," and 4.0 "I feel extremely happy and good"). Thus the greatest effect is less than a single unit on a five-point scale, and most of the differences are even smaller. (The difference between the first two conditions is .2, for example.) With the anger self-report scale, the effects are still smaller, with the mean ranging from 1.39 to 1.91 under the varying experimental conditions. As indicated above, it is not possible to judge the substantive significance of the behavioral index of happiness, because insufficient information is given about the construction of the scale. But for the anger behavioral index, the magnitude of the effects is almost vanishingly small; the range of the mean is from −.18 to 2.28, slightly more than one agreement per subject.

To summarize the results so far, the peripheral manipulations cause small but statistically significant effects on self-evaluated feelings and on emotional behavior. As small as these effects are, they are greater than the effects caused by the epinephrine, since most of the placebo-epinephrine differences are not even statistically significant. How is one to interpret these findings? Before making an attempt, I want to comment on another issue related to magnitude: the absolute magnitude of the intensities of feeling that were under study.

Since Schachter and Singer do not report the separate means for the happiness and anger self-report indices, it might have been difficult to interpret the absolute magnitudes of these indices. In the text, however, the authors indicated that the anger self-report indices were virtually zero, since they suspected that the subjects were unwilling to risk the extra credit grade-points they were being given by indicating anger at the experimenter. The magnitudes of the scales can be interpreted to be almost entirely made up by the happiness units, with a range between 1 (''a little happy'') and 2 (''quite happy'') about 1 unit on a five-point scale. For the behavioral ratings, we cannot interpret the magnitude of the happiness index, but the magnitude of the anger index is also very small, slightly more than one agreement per subject.

I have reviewed Schachter and Singer's findings in some detail because I think that the issue of size of the effects and the levels of intensities in their study has substantive importance for interpreting the implications for the centralist-peripheralist controversy. I interpret their results to mean: for low levels of physiological arousal caused by a stimulant, peripheral variables are more important than the central variable for self-evaluation of subjective response and for emotion-related behavior. This effect is quite small, however, and may only hold if the level of arousal is quite low. Suppose, for example, the intensity of arousal were at the level of "blind rage" or happiness to the point of ecstasy. It seems doubtful that at this level of intensity that information or the social environment would have more effect than physiological arousal. At low intensities of arousal, one has difficulty in locating and interpreting one's feeling: peripheral variables could conceivably be decisive. What I am saying is that the laboratory conditions of the experiment, which lead to very low levels of intensity and small effects, are the very conditions most likely to support the peripheral hypothesis. A much more rigorous test would be under conditions of high intensity and strong changes. Since the theory of repression is mainly concerned with powerful emotions, such as the paralyzing terror of nightmare fear, only a more rigorous testing would be relevant to the theory.

A second limitation in the Schachter and Singer study concerns what seems to be a critical flaw in their analysis, if one seeks to use it as a test of the peripheralist position. Nowhere in their analysis do the authors make any explicit numerical comparisons between the happiness and anger conditions. In terms of the peripheralist argument, the crucial question is, are subjects in the angry social environ-

ment angry and less happy than subjects in the happy social environment, even though their state of physiological
stimulation is the same? The authors' data, or at least their
report of the data, do not give an answer to this question.
They do not compare the self-report indices for the anger
and happiness conditions, and they do not present happiness behavioral indices for the anger conditions, or anger
behavioral indices for the happiness condition. The social
variable is also flawed in another way: there is no control
group for this condition. My conclusion is that the subject's state of information, a peripheral variable, had a
very weak effect on emotional state in both the anger and
happiness condition, but that no effect was found for the
second peripheral variable, the social environment.

Recent formulations have sought to reduce the conflict
between the centralist and peripheral positions by integrating them. Candland (1977, 65–71) has argued for a
"continuous loop" model, in which physiological and
peripheral changes are mutually determining. Such a
model is consonant with the theory of catharsis proposed
here, since it does not eliminate differential physiological
states in fear, grief, and anger, yet allows for important
peripheral effects that are required by the distancing
paradigm. While such an integration is helpful, it does not
solve the main difficulty with existing research and theory
in the area of emotion, from the point of view of my argument: the lack of differentiation between emotional distress and discharge and the lack of precise, systematic
studies of the conditions and effects of discharge. Until a
substantial series of such studies is conducted and their
implications interpreted, the literature on emotions will be
of little help in assessing the theory of catharsis.

Even purely physiological research on emotions is in a
very rudimentary state. Averill (1968), in his review of the
literature on grief, finds the evidence to be meagre and

contradictory. One of the specific issues he explores concerns the basic physiology of grief: does it involve activation of the sympathetic or parasympathetic nervous system? He cites studies and discussions with contradictory interpretations. He himself concludes that the weight of evidence points toward sympathetic activation but warns that his conclusion is quite tentative. He goes on to say that discussion and studies of grief are rare in the psychological literature, probably because the behavior of grieving persons is not explainable within most current models of emotion.

Perhaps the concept of distancing may help in understanding the physiology of grief. Existing studies often make no differentiation between underdistanced grief (hysterical crying), and overdistanced grief (as in clinical depression), and grief at aesthetic distance, as in light or controlled crying. Each of these distances is probably marked by a distinctive physiological process. Using both the distancing concept, and Gellhorn's (1963) model of autonomic processes, I would expect to find underdistanced grief characterized by sympathetic dominance and overdistanced grief by parasympathetic dominance. Extreme cases of under- or over-distancing might involve what Gellhorn calls "runaway" dominance. Grief at aesthetic distance, however, should be marked by what Gellhorn calls the "tuning" of the autonomic nervous system; the rapid alteration between low levels of first sympathetic, then parasympathetic activation.

Conclusion

I will end this chapter by describing several further studies and by giving my assessment of the state of the evidence regarding the theory of catharsis.

Although the crucial distinction between emotional distress and emotional discharge has never been studied directly, there is a study of the crying of infants which may prove to be related. Ostwald and Peltzman (1974) compared the pitch of the crying of normal, possibly brain-damaged, and definitely brain-damaged babies. They found large differences between the three groups; the fundamental frequency of the cry of the normal babies varied in the course of the cry, from beginning to end, between about 440 (Hertz) to about 550; the possibly brain-damaged from about 500 to about 625; and the definitely brain-damaged from about 600 to about 775. If one makes the assumption that the cries of the normal babies, more often than those of the brain-damaged babies, are signals of cathartic crying, and the cries of the brain-damaged babies, more often than the normal babies, are signals of distress, these findings are relevant to the theory of catharsis. This hypothesis could be tested directly by examining the consequences of the different types of cries. If there was found to be, for example, a correlation between pitch and tension, so that low-pitched crying was associated with decreases in tension and high-pitched crying, with increases or constancy of tension, the theory would be supported.

A cross-cultural study which demonstrates the relationship between distress and crying has been reported by Rosenblatt et al. (1976). Using existing studies in the Human Relations Area File, they rated the expression of various kinds of emotions during bereavement in a large number of cultures. One of their findings concerned crying: in seventy-two of seventy-three societies that were rated, crying was found to be present in at least some of the bereaved persons. The only exception was in Balinese society. The authors suggest that even in this society, the impulse to cry is present, but, as with other forms of emotional expression, the Balinese have learned to suppress it. These findings suggest the near-universality of crying in connection with loss and are therefore congruent with the theory of catharsis.

Another report which is indirectly related to the theory of catharsis was published by Rothbart (1973). In reviewing the studies of laughter in infants and children, she suggests that they may be subsumed under the following proposition: "laughter occurs after conditions of heightened tension or arousal when at the same time there is a judgment that the situation is safe or inconsequential." The formulation is exactly parallel to the distancing hypothesis discussed earlier: catharsis occurs when repressed emotion is restimulated in an adequately distanced context, so that both past distress and present safety are experienced equally and simultaneously. That is, if anger or embarassment is restimulated in children in a safe context, as in games or dramas, laughter is likely to occur.

In their review of studies relevant to the catharsis hypothesis, Nichols and Zax describe a study by Symonds (1954) of the most frequent sources of change in psychotherapy. Although they acknowledge that the study provides some support for the theory of catharsis, they raise two objections: Symonds doesn't distinguish between cognitive-emotional and somatic-emotional catharsis, and he doesn't reveal the sources of his cases (Nichols and Zax, 1977, 172). In my judgment, however, these objections do not invalidate Symonds' findings. Since some of his evidence is directly relevant to the theory of catharsis outlined here, I will briefly review his study.

Symonds looked for successful courses of psychotherapy which were traceable to events which occurred during the therapeutic session. He found sixty-eight such cases. He reports that out of the total, "59 followed abreactions, 7 followed interpretations by the therapist, and 2 were related to change in perception which may or may not have been caused by the therapist's comment'' (p. 699).

Symonds argues that his data, as they stand, clearly and forcefully support the hypothesis of therapeutic change as a result of abreaction. He also suggests that his results support the hypothesis even more strongly than is first apparent:

On the basis of these findings, I should like to propose as a hypothesis that all changes in behavior and adjustment occurring as a result of psychotherapy follow abreaction in the therapeutic situation. It is quite possible that in the 9 cases in which the changes apparently followed the therapist's interpretation or were related to changes in the client's perception, the changes actually followed an abreaction that was not noticed or recorded by the therapist, and it is possible that the abreaction might not even have been observable but might have been more in the nature of internal reaction. That is, it is hypothesized that the change took place as a result of the client's abreactive response to the therapist's interpretation or that the shift in perception was accompanied by an abreactive reaction (pp. 699–700).

Symonds goes on to interpret his results in a way that is parallel to the theory proposed here. In seeking to resolve the argument between proponents of insight and proponents of abreaction, he comes up with the following formulation:

Abreaction, however, is dependent on insight in two ways. Before abreaction can take place, the client must perceive the situation in a different way than he is accustomed to perceiving it, that is, as nonthreatening. The shift in perception has been called in this paper Insight I. Abreaction does not have permanent therapeutic value unless it is followed by another type of insight known as Insight II. Insight I is principally a shift in the perception of the other person, namely the therapist. Insight II is principally a shift in the perception of the self.

Insight II depends upon a preceding abreaction which reduces tension, removes threats, and makes the change in perception possible. Insight II paves the way for further abreaction which helps the therapeutic process to proceed until the therapeutic goal is reached (pp. 711–712).

Symonds' argument is precisely parallel to mine. Aesthetic distance (Insight I) is necessary before discharge can occur. Furthermore, after discharge has occurred, the amount of insight increases as a result of the discharge process. Just as Symonds indicates, the initial distance involves an interpretation about the client's relationship to the counselor (or to the audience in the theatre), that is, the relationship is a safe one, and so the second distancing involves insight about the client himself, i.e., new memories and interpretations about distressful events in the past. This is parallel to Symonds' Insight II. Finally, as Symonds indicates in his last two sentences, the more distancing following discharge, the more capable the client is of further discharge. It would seem, therefore, that both Symonds' data and his interpretations support the theory as it has been presented in this book.

The last study I will review is by Borquist, on the effects of crying. This study was not mentioned by Nichols and Zax in their review, probably because it is based on a fairly casual survey and because it is not current. (It was published in 1906.) However, since some of the results can be construed in terms of the concept of distancing, I will provide a brief description.

Borquist conducted a survey on crying behavior in men and women, with 200 respondents. For our purposes, his most relevant finding concerns the effects of crying. Fifty-four of the fifty-seven who responded to the question concerning crying about a specific cause stated the effects were very positive:

F., "If it were not for crying I think people would go insane, not having any way to give vent to their feelings."

F., 18. "I feel as though someone had been talking kind to me and a great load had been taken from me."

F., 23. Speaking of despair, "It was always felt before the crying spell, but never after."

F., 19. "After my crying spell I am sure I felt much relieved. The nervousness was gone and I was ready to enjoy life once more."

Borquist also asked a question about crying without objective cause. The responses to this question were also favorable for the great majority; 71 out of 94 respondents reported favorable effects:

F., 18. "I have an uneasy feeling as though I could not sit down and do anything. After a good cry I feel greatly relieved. It seems as if a great weight had been lifted from me."

F., 21. "I always feel relieved after such a spell, and things generally look bright to me."

F.,— "I have often become so tired, discouraged, or nervous over work and worry that there seemed nothing else to do but have a good cry, and after one has cried a long time relief comes."

F. "A cry sometimes relieves one of that pent up, stuffy feeling and seems to lift a burden that has been resting upon one. Too much repression is bad for the body and the mind both; the mind will not work."

Crying without objective cause may be interpreted to be usually due to unconscious grief. Borquist's results may be construed, therefore, as providing some support for the theory of catharsis offered here. Note, however, that all of the quotations are from women. (The letter F means female, and the next number is age.).

There is one passage in which Borquist appears to anticipate the distancing paradigm which has been discussed here:

An instance of the effect of crying upon the state of tension is related in Tennyson's Princess:

Home they brought her warrior dead;
    She nor swooned nor uttered cry.
All her maidens, watching, said
    "She must weep or she will die."

Then they praised him, soft and low,
    Called him worthy to be loved,
Truest friend and noblest foe;
    Yet she neither spoke nor moved.

Stole a maiden from her place,
    Lightly to the warrior stept
Took the face-cloth from his face;
    Yet she neither moved nor wept.

Rose a nurse of ninety years,
    Set his child upon her knee—
Like a summer tempest came her tears—
    "Sweet my child, I live for thee."

The maidens were wrong in supposing that the outburst could be induced by *increasing* a sense of the bereavement. The experienced nurse knew that it must be diminished.

His analysis corresponds to the distancing paradigm: the princess was overwhelmed by the distress of loss. Tears came only when some of the distress was relieved. The author has observed similar situations in which therapists made use of some elementary dimensions of distancing in determining whether to use "light" (distancing) or "heavy" (removing distance) techniques.

The main dimensions of distancing are present versus past time (the light technique is mentioned first; present time is more distanced, usually, than past time), fiction or fantasy versus reality, rapid review versus detailed recollection, and positive emotions versus negative emotions. That is to say, other things being equal, present-time events, fiction or fantasy, rapid review, and positive emotions are distancing. Past-time events, real events, detailed recollection, and negative or unpleasant events remove distance. Each of these dimensions is indicative of a tactic in managing the distancing of emotions. The therapist who judges a patient to be underdistanced when experiencing an event which is either in the past, real, in detail, and/or negative, may seek to have the patient's attention shifted to events which are in the present, fictional, reviewed rapidly, and/or positive. Two examples will illustrate this technique.

Moving from negative to positive emotions, in a situation of underdistanced grief:

The patient was describing an incident to me in which his father had attacked him with a knife. In the midst of the recollection, the patient becomes visibly distraught. He wrings his hands, stutters, and seems unable to continue. The expression on his face becomes quite sad. He seems to be choking with emotion. I ask: "Were there any good times with your father?" The patient's expression slowly changes to a smile; when he begins to speak "Yes, once he . . .", the patient bursts into tears, and cries for five or ten minutes. After he finishes crying, the patient says that he feels much better, and finishes the story of his father's attack.

Moving from rapid review to detailed recollection, in a situation of overdistanced fear and grief:

The patient tells me a large number of incidents of flashbacks after LSD use. Her tone of voice is expressionless, and she speaks rapidly and abstractly about each event. I interrupt the barrage of incidents, asking her to tell me all the details she can remember about the worst incidents. After describing two incidents in this way, the patient's teeth begin to chatter. She asks me to hold her. In my arms, she shakes violently for two or three minutes and begins to cry somewhat before the shaking stops. After some five minutes of crying, she smiles and begins to laugh and cry happily, at the same time. When she stops, she tells me she feels better than she has in a long time, and wants to know what I did to start her shaking.

These techniques are of course not infallible. In unusual cases, past time may be more distanced than present time, negative emotions more distanced than positive ones, and so on. In most cases, the therapist needs to exercise some ingenuity in assessing the degree of distancing, and trial and error of different techniques of increasing or decreasing distance, until the technique is found that is appropriate to the particular situation. (See the chart "Emotional States and Distance" on p. 65.)

The question which this chapter has addressed, in the main, has been the extent to which the theory of catharsis is supported by evidence. The answer which is suggested by this review, based mostly on Nichols and Zax's work, is that there is virtually no direct evidence, positive or negative, concerning the validity of the theory. There is considerable indirect evidence, however, supporting the theory. This evidence is taken from studies which, for the most part, were conducted for other purposes. The studies of the treatment of pathological mourning, for example, which Nichols and Zax describe, were not conducted for the purpose of testing the theory of catharsis. Their purpose was more practical: to report effective ways of resolving the delay or absence of mourning. These studies therefore represent only limited support for the theory of catharsis. In the absence of direct tests, my judgment is that on balance, existing evidence supports the catharsis hypothesis. In Chapter 7 some studies which seek to test the theory directly are reported.

II. Applications

5.

The Distancing of Emotion in Ritual and Mass Entertainment

Contemporary social science has two seemingly contradictory orientations toward ritual. The positive orientation views ritual, along with myth, as the foundation of all culture—the basis of human consciousness. The negative one sees it as an empty shell, a residue of belief and practices whose functions are lost in an irretrievable past. Both of these traditions are deeply rooted in basic perspectives in anthropology, sociology, and psychology. The purpose of this chapter is to outline a theory of ritual which subsumes both orientations.

The positive theory of ritual was suggested by Durkheim—religious beliefs and practices not only create and sustain the fundamental social structure of a society, but maintain the members' sense of reality. Kluckhohn's (1942, 64) evaluation of this view is representative: "[Myths] have the (to us) scarcely understandable meaningfulness which the tragedies had for the Greek populace. As Matthew Arnold said of these, 'their significance appeared inexhaustible'." Chapple's work (1970) in behavioral anthropology is a strong affirmation of the positive approach to ritual. Chapple indicates that myth and ritual are forms which mediate between social organization and the biological rhythms of human existence. His purview includes not only rituals of the life cycle, the rites of passage at birth, initiation, marriage, and death, but also interaction ritual, which involves the moment-to-moment transitions of daily life. His analysis (p. 304) of the custom of saying grace before a meal is a case in point:

This is a ritual associated with an institutional crisis. . . . Superficially, it may appear incongruous to apply the term, crisis, with all its overtones of emergency, to a group of people assembled to eat a common meal. Yet it is a good case to begin with if we are to understand crises in the institutional sense. . . .

Before the meal is to begin, members of the family have been engaged in other activities . . . adults working, older children being taught . . . women in the kitchen preparing the meal, and younger children playing outside. . . . These now end; the family members come together . . . as a group. . . .

What are the stresses? First . . . the change from one situation to another requires a change in interaction pattern. . . . Second, the transitive properties of human beings make possible the carryover of temperamental reactions into . . . the new adjustments required. . . . Finally, the interaction patterns within the family are reinforced through the . . . interaction forms which the meal specifies. This has emotional benefits as the members return to or begin new relationships. . . .

For Chapple, the ritual of grace facilitates the transition from one social and biological set of rhythms to another, completely different set and in doing so resolves the regularly repeated minor crisis.

Mandelbaum's (1959) analysis of funeral rites illustrates the positive approach to the rituals of the life cycle. He shows how the funeral and the ceremonies of mourning of the Kotas of southern India not only assuage the grief of the bereaved but fulfill important social functions, such as the reinforcement of the order of precedence in the village.

He repeats Firth's (1951, 63) comment with approval: "A funeral rite is a social rite par excellence. Its ostensible object is the dead person, but it benefits not the dead, but the living."

Contrary to these affirmations of the value of ritual, there is a sizable body of opinion that rituals are useless. Turner (1976, 1010) comments: "To those who find not only religious ritual but also marriage ceremonies, funerals and memorial services, initiation ceremonies, and graduation exercises devoid of meaning, it is unclear how ritual could add vitality and reality to anything." Mandelbaum writes of the "deritualization" of American society and Klapp (1969) of the "poverty of ritual." To be sure, some of the thrust of this orientation is directed not to ritual per se, but to the ineffectiveness of ritual in modern societies. Mandelbaum's comments about "deritualization" imply, in part, a comparison of the ineffectiveness of contemporary ritual with its effectiveness in traditional societies. But there is a much darker tone to many statements.

Freud in one of his later papers (1948, 35) likened ritual to the obsessional symptoms of the neurotic patient: ". . . one might venture to regard the obsessional neurosis as a pathological counterpart to the formation of a religion, to describe this neurosis as a private, religious system, and a religion as a universal obsessional neurosis." Even Malinowski (1931, 639), who celebrates the significance of ritual, flirts with a similar idea: "Fear moves every human being to aimless but compulsory acts; in the presence of an ordeal one always has recourse to obsessive daydreaming." He goes on to make the point that ritual serves to allay anxiety in those areas of a culture in which there is great uncertainty. Although Malinowski is a supporter of ritual, the underlying thought is quite negative, since it suggests that ritual has as little value for society as the symptoms of obsessive neurosis have for the suffering neurotic.

Goffman (1971, 62) gives the curtest definition of ritual in the negative tradition: "Ritual is a perfunctory, conventionalized act through which an individual portrays his respect and regard for some object of ultimate value. . . ." The operative idea in this definition is not that individuals have objects of ultimate value but that the ritual act is perfunctory and conventionalized.

The formulation by Geertz of religion as a symbolic system follows the negative tradition in its outlines. He argues that religion attempts to cope with the ungovernable forces in human experience: ignorance, pain, and injustice. Geertz sees some utility in religious symbolism, since it establishes long-lasting motives toward the real world. Like Malinowski and Freud, however, he views the emotional components of religion, which he considers to be the creation of pervasive moods, as ephemeral: "Motives have a directional cast, they describe a certain overall course, gravitate toward certain, usually temporary, consummations. But moods vary only as to intensity: they go nowhere. . . . Like fogs, they just settle and drift; like scents, suffuse and evaporate" (Geertz, 1965, 208). This treatment of the emotional component of religion seems to me characteristic of the modern temper in social science, alienated both from ritual and from emotion.

As indicated in Chapter 1, myth and ritual have been systematically investigated by Lévi-Strauss (1969), Turner (1967), Firth (1972), Douglas (1970), and many others. Their analyses emphasize cognitive and verbal aspects, however, to the virtual exclusion of emotions. Lévi-Strauss, Firth, and Douglas, for the most part, ignore the affective components. Even Turner, who is more sensitive to some of the emotional elements in ritual, considers emotions in a global, undifferentiated, and, therefore, quite superficial way. None of these authors indexes any of the main emotions I shall discuss: grief, fear, shame, and anger.

I believe that the de-emphasis of emotion found in the work of Malinowski, later Freud, Geertz, and other social theorists is part of a rationalistic bias which gives undue emphasis to cognitive elements. Such a perspective is also ethnocentric, since it derogates that aspect of ritual which Western culture effectively deals with, through knowledge and science, and ignores that part—emotion—which our culture handles poorly if at all. I shall argue that ritual can perform a vital function: the appropriate distancing of emotion. I shall propose a theory of ritual and its associated myth as dramatic forms for coping with universal emotional distresses.

Ritual Management of Distress

In the game of "peek-a-boo," the mother first hides her face with her hands; then she removes her hands, moving her smiling face toward the baby, and says "Peek-a-boo!" This cycle is repeated over and over. If the mother's timing is right, the baby will begin to laugh each time she shows her face. If she hides too long, the game is spoiled; the baby may cry or become frightened. If she does not hide long enough, the baby will not become sufficiently aroused to laugh.

This game contains, in a simple form, the three necessary elements for the successful ritual management of distress: (1) the evocation of the distress (that of separation); (2) a distancing device (the baby knows that the mother has not really gone); and (3) the discharge of the distress (the baby laughs). (For another interpretation of peek-a-boo, see Maurer, 1967.) These three elements are characteristic of many types of ritual, including various forms of funeral rites and curing rituals.

The ritual which most clearly contains the elements found in the game of peek-a-boo is the vastly elaborated set of rites concerned with life after death. These rituals and myths are centered around the distress of separation caused by death; the distancing device is the complex of beliefs and practices which indicate that the deceased person is not actually lost forever, and the discharge of distress usually takes the form of weeping. As in peek-a-boo, if the conditions are right, the mourners may attain sufficient distance from their distress that discharge may take place, in this case, in the form of weeping. The distancing paradigm outlined in Chapter 3 can be used to understand the dynamics of ritual and its contemporary surrogate, mass entertainment. These forms provide at least the possibility for occasions of repeated catharsis, in the ceremonial occasions and times of entertainment, in daily living, for all members of a society, not just those in treatment. To understand the reason why repeated abreaction might be necessary it is necessary to consider processes which give rise to the accumulation of distressful emotion.

The Accumulation of Repressed Emotion

The need for repeated abreactions suggests a much larger reservoir of repressed emotion than was envisioned by Freud and Breuer. The accumulation of repressed emotion depends upon two distinct processes, the generation of distress, on the one hand, and the blockage of discharge, on the other.

Repeated episodes of overwhelming distress are unavoidable even in the course of what appears to be the most normal life. Grief, for example, as a result of intense and incommunicable feelings of separation and loss, would appear to be an inescapable feature of infancy. It was previously suggested (in Chapter 3) that the infant's ability to form objects, and attachments to those objects, which are separate from the self depends in a vital way upon crying. Tomkins (1963) argues that to the extent that the infant is able to cry about a lost object, and therefore work through the loss, it will be able to risk attachment in the future. Obversely, if the infant is unable to resolve the loss, it will be unwilling to risk attachment.

A similar argument has been made in Chapter 3 on the prevalence of fear and anger, that is, that fear is generated by danger to life and anger by frustration. Since the infant is unable to cope with separation, a brief separation from his mother can generate grief, fear, or anger. These responses are reactions to separation from adults, who are the infant's only source of support. Finally, embarrassment is more or less continuously generated, particularly in childhood, in the learning and performance of innumerable nuances of cultural forms, for example, the proper pronunciation and usage of language.

The second process responsible for the accumulation of repressed emotion is the blockage of discharge. Even distress which is communicable will usually not be completely discharged because of the strong external and internal controls on discharge. External controls occur because we all learn to do work on others to suppress discharge. Children who are discharging may be told, "Don't be a crybaby," "Be a man," "Temper, temper, young lady," "Go to your room until you can come out with a smile on your face," "If you don't stop crying, I'll give you something to cry about," or some variant of these phases. Probably more important than these are nonverbal gestures of anger, impatience, threat, ridicule, or embarrassment.

Adults who are crying, shaking, screaming or laughing in excess of the very stringent social limits for these activities may be told to take a drink or a tranquilizer or to see a psychiatrist.

In the face of the punitive response to discharge, children develop internal blocks that interfere with their emotional expression. A boy who is hurt learns very quickly to hide his crying from his peers. Initially he is able to delay tears until he is alone. After thousands of repetitions, however, the process is overlearned. He blocks the tears so well that he forgets how to cry. The prohibition against crying may be less severe with girls, but it is still operative. The discharge of anger is much more negatively sanctioned in girls than in boys, with the result that many women have forgotten how to feel or express anger.

To recapitulate, emotional distress is unavoidably and repeatedly generated in the process of living, for both children and adults. Since there are usually powerful external and internal controls on the discharge of this distress, most persons accumulate repressed emotion. In traditional societies, it seems likely that ritual, with its associated myth, provided a context that was both a psychologically enabling and a socially acceptable occasion for repeated catharsis.

Ritual and Distancing

Given our discussion of catharsis and distancing, it is possible to define ritual, not only in terms of its object, as Durkheim did, but in terms of the emotional dynamics of the participants. For the purpose of this chapter, I will define ritual as the potentially distanced reenactment of situations of emotional distress that are virtually universal in a given culture. As indicated above, there are three cen-

on: recurring shared emotional
, and discharge.

around recurring sources of
of temporary separation gives
as the pain of permanent loss
ieral rites and ceremonies of
ı one social status to another,

the pain of loss of one's old rela-
tionships and the fear connected with one's apprehensions
about the new status, which lead to the rites of passage.
The ceremony of greeting, perhaps, is a ritual which co-
heres around the fear and embarrassment of making contact with others, particularly strangers. Ritual drama, as in
the case of Greek tragedy, is concerned with the universal
human distresses: death, injustice, betrayal, exile.

Any device which allows people to be both participants
in, and observers of, their own distress accomplishes the
second component in this conception of ritual, distancing.
Belief in an afterlife has already been mentioned. The
ritual of prayer exactly distances the communicant so that
he or she is as much participant as observer, so long as the
communicant both believes and disbelieves that he or she
is in communication with a supernatural being. This double vision, of both believing and not believing simultaneously, which is characteristic of participants in living
ritual, may be the source of the puzzlement that marks the
notes of many ethnographers when they describe the myths
of cultures other than their own. For aesthetic distance, the
communicant must both believe and disbelieve. From the
point of view of the theory outlined here, the communicant
who is both participant and observer can experience repressed emotion and discharge it.

One example of a very ordinary distancing device is

the language of parting. In most languages, there is a phrase of parting which is indicative of a presumably permanent separation: "farewell," "adieu," "vaya con Dios." In most modern societies, however, these phrases are seldom used. The almost universally used salutation, even for permanent separations, is one that intimates temporary leave-taking: "I'll be seeing you," "hasta la vista," "auf Wiedersehen." When the separation is in fact permanent, these latter salutations are distancing devices: the participants can both believe that the separation is temporary and disbelieve it.

In curing rites, the belief in possession by spirits can be seen as a distancing device. In the case of the exorcism reported by Obeyesekere (1970), it is ostensibly not Alice Nona who complains bitterly about her husband's failings but the Lord Vishnu, who has possessed her body. To the extent that she simultaneously believes and disbelieves that she is possessed, Alice Nona can maintain the proper distance for catharsis. This is not to say that subjects of exorcism may not occasionally almost totally believe that they are possessed. According to the theory, however, if this happens the exorcism will not be therapeutic, since the experience will be almost completely underdistanced.

By far the most common situation in modern ritual, however, is not underdistancing, the return of unbearable emotion, but overdistancing, the absence of any emotion. It is in this sense that the theory proposed here subsumes both negative and positive orientations toward ritual. The negative orientation, expressed as statements about the death of God, the poverty of ritual, deritualization, peremptoriness, or meaninglessness, focuses on one extreme of the distancing continuum, overdistancing. The positive orientation, on the other hand, seems to assume another fixed point of distancing, aesthetic distance. It is noteworthy that there is little criticism of ritual as underdistanced—total absorption to the point that the participants leave the ceremony more tense than when they began. Such criticism exists: statements deploring the participant's total involvement in the rituals of voodoo, the snake-handling cults, and some of the ecstatic fundamentalist churches are cases in point, but they are rare.

Ritual and Catharsis

I will consider some evidence connecting ritual, catharsis, and a sense of well-being in two areas: funeral rites and curing rituals.

Gorer (1965, 126) has made the point that English society has virtually no mourning ritual: "I think that the material presented has . . . demonstrated that the . . . British people are . . . without adequate guidance as to how to treat death and bereavement and without social help in living through . . . the grief and mourning which are the inevitable responses in human beings to the death of someone whom they have loved." He argues that there are important social consequences of the denial of mourning, such as increasing public callousness toward the loss of human life and a preoccupation with violence in the mass media. Pincus (1976, 173–174) also points to the denial of mourning and, through the use of case histories, shows that unexpressed grief gives rise to serious individual problems: "The four cases discussed in this chapter are examples of failures to mourn. In each of them, unresolved grief led to a defense against emotional commitment, a denial of feeling, and an impoverishment of the personality." Although she focuses her attention on the personal and interpersonal sources of the failure to mourn, her case histories are full of material supporting Gorer's argument: the absense of adequate bereavement myth and ritual in modern society deprives the survivors of the opportunity to mourn.

Insofar as a picture can be reconstructed of mourning in classical and preliterate societies, the case was certainly different. It would seem that myth and ritual provided a framework for catharsis. Weeping was encouraged and accepted. In the case of the Quechan, a California Indian tribe, "crying is expected of one. Only by allowing yourself to let go of your emotions do they know how badly you feel for the family. . . . The room is filled with tears, men and women joining together paying their respects. This begins four days of mourning" (Swift Arrow, 1974, 23). Like the Quechan, most traditional societies have a defined period of weeping, as is the case in traditional Jewish communities: "The second stage of mourning represents the first three days of the seven-day period (the Shiva), which begins after the funeral. These three days are devoted to unrestrained weeping and lamentation" (Pollock, 1972, 11). Many traditional societies have a special place marked off, as well as a definite period, for weeping. In the Bara culture of Madagascar, callers are received in a hut called the "house of many tears": "The closest kinswomen begin to cry and the others gradually join in, the most recently arrived mourners joining earliest and most vehemently. As they wail the women cover their heads and faces, put their hands on one another's backs" (Huntington, 1973, 67). It would appear that public mourning was common in classic Greek society, in connection both with funeral rites and tragic drama (Lucas, 1968, 273):

Since pity, especially in tragedy, is often pity for the dead or the bereaved, it is akin to the shared or public lamentation which is part of life in small closely knit communities. . . . [There is a suggestion] that the audience luxuriated in community sorrow, "surrendering itself" to lamentation and taking part in the mourning along with actors and chorus.

The image of the audience "luxuriating" in sorrow is important for our purposes, since it suggests that the crying was not underdistanced but occurred at aesthetic distance. The idea of mourning occurring through a type of weeping that is not unpleasant is suggested by the language of some of the surviving ritual laments, such as those of the Trojan women (Alexiou, 1974, 125):

> How good are tears, how sweet are dirges,
> I would rather sing dirges than eat or drink.
> How sweet are tears to those of evil fortune,
> and the weeping of dirges, and the sorrowful Muse.

These materials suggest that traditional societies have mourning rituals which give rise to cathartic weeping at aesthetic distance.

A similar case for the catharsis of fear can be made in the case of curing rituals. Shaking and sweating, as well as explicit references to subjective feelings of fear, characterize many of the descriptions of curing ritual. An example is provided by Katz's (1973) description of curing in the !Kung Bushman tribe:

then you start to shiver. . . . N/um [the energy or spirit evoked by the curing ritual] makes you tremble . . . . Emotions are aroused to an extraordinary level, whether they be fear or exhilaration . . . (p. 140).

Along with feelings of release and liberation, !kia [curing ritual] also brings profound feelings of pain and fear (p. 143).

You start shivering . . . and you will be trembling like leaves in the winds . . . (pp. 147–148).

Shaking is also described in the curing rituals of other cultures, as in descriptions of the Zar cult in Iran (Modaressi, 1968, 154) and the Umbanda in Brazil (Figge,

1975, 248–249). Shaking is documented for the curing ceremonies of several cultures by Sargent (1974, 126–127, 135, 145, 169). These descriptions must be interpreted cautiously, since it is not possible to determine from them whether the shaking is the involuntary autonomic response required by my theory, or voluntary movements standing in relation to involuntary shivering and sweating, as wailing (a voluntary expressive action) stands to sobbing with tears (an involuntary response).

The sweating that accompanies the curing ritual is emphasized in another paper on the !Kung: "Sweat (cho) is the most important of the trance symbols, for it is the palpable and visible expression of medicine on the surface of the body. . . . The production and transmission of sweat is the key element in the curing ritual" (Lee, 1968, 44). Since the !Kung ritual involves energetic dancing, it is unclear to what extent the sweating is due to the heat of the dance rather than to an autonomic fear discharge. This ambiguity is removed in the case of the curing ritual of the Balahis in India, since the sweating occurs in participants who are not dancing, but only swaying gently on their heels: "His whole body begins to shake and tremble, and sweat pours out of his pores" (Fuchs, 1964, 132). In this case at least, the curing ritual is clearly and unambiguously marked by the indicators of fear discharge at aesthetic distance that are proposed by this theory.

These fragments from ethnographic materials in no way demonstrate my thesis; they merely serve to illustrate it. They show that the theory predicts features of the data, such as the profuse sweating of the participants in the Balahis curing rites, and the association of weeping and pleasure in the Greek lamentations, which would otherwise be surprising.

Modern forms of mass entertainment also evoke extreme emotional responses in their audiences. The romantic tragedies that make up most daytime serials touch upon many themes, but the central emotional component usually is some form of grief, brought on by loss through death, injury, or separation. *Love Story* is a recent exemplar of this genre in film. The dramas of suspense, violence, horror, terror, and disaster all evoke strong reactions of fear or anxiety in audiences. *Jaws,* a film which produces reactions of terror, was in its time the greatest financial success in film history, having earned more than the prior champion, *Gone with the Wind.* Horror films like *The Exorcist* and *The Omen* were also extremely popular. Disaster films like *The Towering Inferno, Earthquake, Airport,* and *The Poseidon Adventure* also evoke fear. The size of the audience and the amount of viewing time of television dramas of violence such as "SWAT," "The Rookies," "Starsky and Hutch," "Baretta," "Kojak," and "Hawaii Five-O" probably make violence the most popular of the forms considered here. Suspense films, such as *Sleuth* and *Marathon Man,* also evoke fear.

Dramas of violence and suspense probably evoke a somewhat more complex set of emotions in audiences than do the disaster, terror, and horror dramas. These latter dramas involve threats to life and limb from natural and supernatural forces—earthquake, fire, sharks, or the devil, and therefore probably evoke only one emotion: fear. The dramas of violence and suspense, however, involve threats between human beings. To the extent that the audience identifies with the victims of violence, these dramas also evoke responses of fear. But to the extent that the audience identifies with the perpetrators of violence, the largest emotional response is probably anger. This is to say that dramas of violence evoke both fear and anger, with fear probably predominating. In some types, however, such as those which emphasize revenge (*Straw Dogs, Death Wish, Taxi Driver*), anger probably predominates.

Some of these entertainment forms generate unique emotional responses from special audiences. Films like *Shaft* and *Superfly*, which feature black heroes beating and killing whites, appear to evoke strong reactions of anger in black audiences. *Harold and Maude* and, to a lesser extent, films like *If*, which concern violent rebellion against adults, appear to evoke similar reactions in audiences of young people. Films of male brutality to women, and their revenge, like *Lipstick*, evoke anger from audiences of women.

The emotional reaction of audiences to sports contests, game shows, and comedy is not as intuitively obvious as the forms already discussed. It is probably true that in contact sports, such as football, wrestling, and boxing, there is a component of fear and perhaps anger, as in the case of the dramas of violence already mentioned. But what about baseball, basketball, tennis, and golf, which attract huge audiences and have little or no violence? I will argue that the main emotion in spectator sports involves the dimension of triumph, at the positive end of the continuum, and humiliation, at the negative end. Audiences identify with the competing teams or individuals and feel triumph with winning and humiliation with losing. The emotion of humiliation is closely related to, or even may be considered to be identical to, what I have called shame and embarrassment.

I think this same emotional dimension is also the major audience reaction to game shows. Rather than winning honor, as in sports contests, the competitors in game shows win material possessions, allowing audiences to vicariously experience triumph and humiliation. This interpretation of game shows is similar to Ruth Benedict's analysis of the emotional dynamics of the Kwakiutl society, in *Patterns of Culture* (1934), already discussed in Chapter 1. She argued that just as the main dimension of emotion in the Dobu society was fear (of sorcery), the main dimension in Kwakiutl society involved triumph or humiliation. She pointed to the Potlatch as the focal institution for the Kwakiutls, in which one either humiliated, or was humiliated, through demonstrations of the relative size of one's material possessions.

Both competitive sports and game shows involve the phenomenon of losing face. In sports one loses face by losing the game and in game shows by losing material possessions. Comedy is also based, in part, upon losing face, but in an entirely different way, Face is lost by comic characters, not by losing honor in games or losing possessions, but by making public mistakes. Social gaffes, blunders, and boners are central threads of comedy. Falling on a banana peel, mispronouncing a word, garbling a phrase, mistaking a lamp for a person (*Mr. Magoo*), or tying your shoe to a bedpost are mistakes which provide the ingredients of comedy. In classical comedy, one particular type of mistake virtually established the genre, that of mistaken identity. Whether mistaking one identical twin for another (*Comedy of Errors*), or mistaking a man for a woman (*Charlie's Aunt*), mistaken identity makes up the sole plot and occasion for humor in many classic comedies.

In both classic and contemporary comedy, the other emotional foundation for humor is anger. Slapstick and cartoon humor contains a very high percentage of violent or aggressive acts. *Tom and Jerry*, the *Roadrunner* cartoons, and comedy routines such as those in the *Three Stooges* contain a few episodes of humor based on mis-

127

takes, but most of the incidents are acts of aggression. A single *Roadrunner* cartoon usually contains enough mayhem to fill a hospital, if the characters were flesh-and-blood humans rather than fantasy animals. The issue of cartoon violence has caused some contention among the researchers studying the impact of televised violence, since it is unclear whether the violence in cartoons should be counted or not. I will return to this issue in my later discussion of distancing devices.

Emotion and the Poverty of Ritual

As already indicated, ritual also is related to collective emotion. All cultures have funeral and mourning rites which deal, in part, with the grief caused by death. Rituals which deal with fear are no longer familiar to us, but in most cultures, religious rites often concern the management of fear, as in the case of the curing rites described above. The intimations of universal disaster now evoked by films like *Earthquake* were once commonly held feelings in Christian congregations, associated with the Day of Judgment. The belief in eternal damnation (in hell-fire and brimstone) was once a central preoccupation with entire communities in Christian countries. Whole religions, such as the Shakers and the Quakers, arose out of collective expressions of fear and anxiety. Ritual dramas, such as classic Greek drama, deal with all of the collective distresses: grief growing out of death and exile, the fear of death and defeat, rage at frustration and injustice, and the shame and humiliation of dishonor.

In modern society, the connection between strong emotion and ritual appears to have been severed. The loss of emotional vitality in ritual has been variously described. Klapp (1969) speaks of "the poverty of ritual," and Mandelbaum (1959) of the "deritualization" of American society. Goffman (1971) goes so far as to define ritual as a perfunctory and conventionalized act. In the religious sphere, the term "secularization" is used to refer both to the decreasing emotional meaning of religious rites ("desacralization") and to the decreasing influence of religion on life of communities (Schneider, 1970, 175–184). Data on participation by church members collected by Stark and Glock (1968) can be interpreted to mean that, despite widespread stated belief in God, actual emotional and physical involvement in churches is, to use Goffman's term, perfunctory. The recent "God is dead" episode was a literary reflection of increasing deritualization.

O'Dea's views are representative:

Present-day worship involves symbolic complexes that arose in previous periods of history . . . [which] reflect in some degree social and psychological conditions which no longer exist. They arose in response to needs that were to some extent specific to the culture and society of the time. How adequate are such symbolic complexes to the expressive needs of people in modern Western societies . . . ? . . . there is reason to believe that much symbolism loses its resonance, that it "wears out" and becomes alienated from the interior religious dispositions of people. Can it be revived, or must new symbolic vehicles be discovered? (O'Dea, 1970, 258).

In the discussion that follows, I will refer to the contemporary "wearing out" of the emotional resonance of ritual, and its associated myths and symbols, by using Klapp's phrase, the poverty of ritual. Most theorists argue that the poverty of ritual is always associated with the loss of community, and some theorists argue that the poverty of ritual is one of the fundamental causes of the loss of community.

It can be argued that the rise of mass entertainment and the increasing poverty of ritual are both products and causes of the same process, the increasing repression of emotional distress in modern societies. To explain this process, it is first necessary to review the model of the ritual management of emotional distress alluded to in the discussion above.

Ritual is necessarily a complex event, serving many functions. One of the functions frequently noted in the anthropological literature is the reaffirmation of the hierarchical structure of a given society. Funerals, among the things that they do, reaffirm the hierarchical position of priests, village headman, and so on. These functions obviously have nothing to do with the emotional needs of the bereaved.

However, ritual usually does serve emotional needs, as well. To see the emotional function of ritual, it is useful to look at a more elementary social form—those children's games whose sole purpose seems to be emotional. I am thinking of games such as tickling, peek-a-boo (previously mentioned), and peer games such as "Simon Says." In these games, we can see in high relief the components that are necessary for the ritual management of distress.

In his comments on the game of tickling, Koestler points to what might be generalized to be a model of the ritual of emotion: " . . . tickling a child will call out a wriggling and squirming response. But the child will laugh only—and this is the crux of the matter—if an additional condition is fulfilled; it must perceive the tickling as a *mock attack,* a caress in a mildly aggressive disguise" (1964, 80). The three major elements in Koestler's explanation of tickling are: first, the idea of an *attack;* second, the idea that the attack is not real, but a *mock* attack; and third, the outcome of the mock attack, *laughter*. That is, tickling will produce laughter if, and only if, it is perceived as a mock attack. Koestler goes on to explore two ways that tickling can fail: you cannot tickle yourself successfully—the element of mock is too great, and the element of attack too small. Conversely, the mother of the baby is much more successful at getting her baby to laugh than a stranger. With a stranger, the element of mock is perceived as too small, the element of attack too great. (Similar results have been obtained in a study in which comparisons were made between mothers tickling with and without masks. It was found that mothers without masks were more successful—again, when the mothers were wearing masks, the element of mock may have been too small and the element of attack too large.)

The peer games that older children play, such as "Simon Says," can be considered to involve the participants in perceiving the game as a form which produces mock mistakes. There are a large number of similar games, such as "The Elephant and the Palm Tree," "Red Light, Green Light," and "Mother, May I?," all of which have rules that guarantee a large number of mistakes. In "Simon Says," commands are given by the child taking the part of the leader in such a way (e.g., rapidly) that the other participants will make mistakes, that is, they will obey commands not prefaced by the phrase "Simon Says," which usually results in laughter. These types of games can be spoiled by too much of the element of mockery, such as lifeless commands by the leader, or by too little mockery, as with curt commands that are too much like those issued by a real-life authority figure.

In Koestler's analysis, the common thread that would unite these three games—tickling, peek-a-boo, and mistake games—is what he calls *bisociation,* the simultaneous experience of a situation "in two (internally) self-consistent but habitually incompatible frames of reference" (35). Koestler goes on to apply this idea to tickling: "It is probably the first situation encountered in life which

131

makes the infant live on two planes at once, the first delectable experience in bisociation—a foretaste of the pleasures to come at the pantomime show, of becoming a willing victim to the illusions of the stage, of being tickled by the horror-thriller . . . the tickled child's laughter is the discharge of apprehensions recognized as unfounded by the intellect'' (81). Implicit in Koestler's comments is the generalization that any situation which gives rise to a precisely balanced experience of distress on the one hand, and safety on the other, will result in laughter.

Our analysis of the childhood games of tickling, peek-a-boo, and mistake games fits very well into the distancing paradigm. These games can be spoiled through underdistancing, as when the stranger, rather than the mother, tickles the child, restimulating too much distress at too little distance, or when the mother hides her face too long, or the leader in a mistake game makes the commands and ridicule of mistakes too much like real life. On the other hand, these games can also be spoiled by overdistancing: one cannot tickle oneself, the mother doesn't hide her face long enough to arouse the baby, or the commands of the leader in a mistake game are slow and lifeless; the distance is too great, and the amount of distress restimulated too small. The theory of distancing outlined here subsumes and broadens Koestler's analysis of the mixture of the elements of mockery and distress that produce bisociation and laughter.

There is one way in which the theory of distancing fails to fit several of the games described above, however. If the theory as stated were correct, then only the mistake and tickling games, when properly played, would produce laughter. The theory predicts that games like "Simon Says," which generate public errors, should restimulate repressed embarrassment and, therefore, cause laughter.

Similarly, the tickling game, which restimulates the distress of being attacked, might restimulate fear and anger. Since laughter is one of the signals of the catharsis of anger, this game, at least in part, can be explained by the theory. However, the theory also predicts that tickling should restimulate repressed fear and cause, therefore, shivering and cold sweat. At the time of this writing, there is no evidence that this is the case. Furthermore, the peek-a-boo game fits the theory even less well. If peek-a-boo restimulates repressed grief, then crying, rather than laughing, should result from a well-played game. Clearly, the theory, as it has been stated so far, is incomplete, since it explains the results of tickling only incompletely and of peek-a-boo not at all.

An additional provision may be needed in the theory. Suppose that most distressful episodes contain all, or almost all, of the distressful emotions. When a parent unexpectedly slaps a child's face, the child probably feels, in addition to pain, at least some grief, fear, anger, and embarrassment. When the distress of such an attack is restimulated, any one of these emotions may be discharged. Since laughter is the least negatively sanctioned of the forms of catharsis and, therefore, the least deeply repressed, it is the form of discharge that is obtained first and most easily. This theory predicts, therefore, a somewhat surprising and as yet untested result: if the tickling and peek-a-boo games are played to the hilt, there should be further forms of catharsis after laughter has occurred— perhaps shivering and sweating and, in the case of peek-a-boo, crying. This provision is supported by observations on normal bereavement. Several studies suggest that bereavement entails a number of phases marked by different emotions. Persons who have lost a loved one through death not only go through a phase of intense grief, but also a phase of anger. Hinton (1967, 170–172) reviews six studies which report this finding. Perhaps systematic observations of bereavement would show still further phases of fear and embarrassment. Fear over the realization that one might die oneself, or humiliation at having lost a loved one, or triumph at having oneself survived, are reactions of bereavement that are not unknown among next-of-kin.

Distancing Devices

For effective ritual management of distress, ritual forms are necessary which produce two quite different effects: first, the evocation of collectively held repressed emotion and, second, a context which insures optimal distancing of that distress, so that catharsis can occur. We will limit the remaining discussion to the second problem, optimal distancing.

Distancing devices are used to introduce (or, in some cases, to reduce) what Koestler would call the mock element, in games, rituals, and entertainment. Distancing devices in psychotherapy were discussed in Chapter 4. In the games we have mentioned, the distancing devices lead to the player's perception that the game is not ordinary reality but only a parody. In tickling, for example, the distancing devices are those characteristics of the tickler's manner which signal that a real attack is not occurring: the lightness or even absence of touch, the smiling, rather than angry, countenance, and the playful sounds and phrases ("I'm going to get you") which distinguish tickling from a real attack. Similarly, in peek-a-boo, the distancing device is the manner of playing the game which gives almost continual assurance to the child that the mother only appears to be, but is not really, gone.

There are innumerable kinds of distancing devices, and they are, at least in part, each unique to a particular social form. However, it is possible to characterize in an abstract way some of the most prominent features of devices which are shared by many different forms.

In ritual, among the most primitive devices which serve to regulate emotional distance are beliefs and practices concerning supernatural beings. Under ideal conditions, collective beliefs and practices oriented toward the supernatural may serve exactly to distance an audience, by allowing its members to be both participants in and observers of distressful emotion. As an example, consider an audience which is engaged in collective prayer, concerning the loss of a loved one. For this prayer to be effective in the ritual management of distress, the present theory requires that the members of the audience be both devout believers and unabashed skeptics, simultaneously. To the extent that the congregation believes it is in the hands of a loving god, to that extent members of the group become observers of their distressful emotions. But to the extent that they do not believe, to that extent they are participants in those emotions.

A similar analysis has already been made of belief in the afterlife. To the extent that the group believes that death will result in permanent loss, to that extent the group will experience profound grief; but to the extent that the group believes in an afterlife, the separation is only temporary; there is no occasion for grief. Belief in an afterlife can be seen as an adult version of the game of peek-a-boo, played out on a cosmic scale. The lost one is both present and absent, simultaneously, like the mother in peek-a-boo. The paradox of this analysis is that rituals may become emotionally impoverished because of either too little belief, or too much. For bisociation to occur, members of the group must be both skeptics and believers. To the extent that belief and disbelief are exactly balanced in an area which involves repressed emotion, to that extent catharsis can occur.

A device which serves to distance emotion that is common to games, rituals, and entertainment is emotional contagion in crowds, or, as this process is called in current studies of the psychology of laughter, social facilitation (Chapman and Foot, 1976). Repressed emotion which is evoked in a group setting is ordinarily more distanced than when the same process occurs in isolated individuals. The mere presence of others serves to keep at least part of the individual's attention in the present, focused on the other persons. Furthermore, collective catharsis is facilitative: the laughter of the others signals to the individual that permission is given to laugh; the normal rules which serve to repress emotional discharge are relaxed. An individual who is crying in the presence of others who are also crying is more able to be both a participant in, and an observer of, his or her own distress. It is in respect to social facilitation that television is the least advantageous form of mass entertainment for the purposes of catharsis. The laugh track on situation comedies is an attempt to remedy this situation, but it is unclear whether it has any effect. Compared to theatre, sports contests, or even films, viewers of television are relatively isolated and, therefore, less likely to experience the balanced laughing, crying, or other forms of discharge that occur at aesthetic distance.

Dramatic techniques which provide audiences with an immediate, realistic portrayal of experiences like those of the audience, and with characters who are similar to the members of the audience, increase the likelihood of the restimulation of repressed emotion in all members of the audience and decrease the likely distance of the members of the audience from their emotions. Similarly, any technique which makes the dramatic action less immediate, real, or similar to the experiences of the members of the audience increases the distance.

One very straightforward way to regulate emotional distance is through the regulation of apparent physical distance. The apparent (or Hall) distance from the viewer at which the action takes place influences the emotional distance.[1] All things being equal, the less the physical distance, the less the emotional distance. For this reason, film can be used in a way that is extremely underdistanced as compared to theatre or other live entertainment, since film can use very short Hall distances and very large images, so that the action appears to the viewers to be taking place (psychologically) right in their laps. Television would fall somewhere between film and live entertainment, since it can use short Hall distances, but cannot use "larger-than-life" projected images. The greater the Hall distance or the smaller the image, the greater the likelihood that the audience's experience will not be underdistanced, since the long apparent distance from the action, and the small images, are a constant reminder to members of the audience that they are observers and not participants.

Among the distancing devices used in dramatic forms, musical cueing is perhaps the single most powerful, and at the same time, the most unobtrusive. Music seems particularly important in generating tension and suspense in the various forms of fear dramas. In the film *Jaws*, the arousal of the fear of the shark is continually insinuated by a bass motif in the score. Music also plays an important part in romantic tragedies. The film *Adele H.* seemed flat and uninvolving to many viewers, although it was unclear to them why this was the case. The director, Truffaut, had

---

1. The Hall distance is the apparent distance between the viewer and the image. The larger the image, the shorter the apparent distance.

intentionally omitted all musical cueing. Most audiences have become so dependent on emotional prompting from a musical score that they didn't know how to react to the film. The way in which the various components of music evoke and distance emotions is much too complex to be treated in this paper. A beginning analysis can be found in *Emotion and Meaning in Music,* by Meyer (1956).

Perhaps the broadest and most important types of distancing devices are the techniques I will refer to as stylization. Any dramatic technique which reminds the audience that the action is not real increases the distance. The use of masks by characters in primitive dramas is an example. Animated cartoons are perhaps the corresponding contemporary device. The characters are not accurately drawn but are caricatures of human beings or animals which parody humans. These characters do not closely resemble humans, nor do they shed blood or feel pain. However, a single distancing device, such as animation, does not always completely control emotional distance, since other factors, such as the realism of the distressful situation, the music, or the voice-overs, may override the animation. In the case of some of the early Disney animations, like *Bambi* or *Dumbo,* many children apparently experienced underdistanced distress, even though the characters were extremely stylized.

In classical drama, stylized speech and other dramatic conventions affect distance. Rhyme and meter, for example, serve to remind the audience that the dramatic action is not real, as do asides and soliloquies. Some of Shakespeare's characters move from meter to natural speech and back again, in a way which suggests an attempt on the playwright's part to affect audience distance.

Plots which give the characters mythic or fictional dimensions increase distance through stylization. Historical dramas move the action to the past and science fiction to the future. Cowboy dramas have more distance than police stories, because the characters are less real to contemporary urban audiences. Himmelweit, in her study of the effects of television violence on children, found that violence in Western dramas did not frighten children, but that violence in detective dramas did (1958, 193–210).

Disruption of the time frame is another contemporary technique for stylizing drama that increases distance. Flashbacks remind the audience that they are observers, since the dramatic action does not unfold in chronological time. The film *Violins du Bal* is a recent essay on how to use the time frame to provide a distance from distressing autobiographical events.

Any device which provides an abstraction of a distressful event, rather than rich, multidimensional images, increases the distance through stylization. The classic device of having violence occur offstage, and then reporting it only verbally, is a familiar example. Furthermore, the verbal description of a distressful event may itself be more or less stylized through abstraction. To have a character report that the king has been murdered is much more distanced than a long and detailed description of exactly how the murder took place. Other things being equal, the briefer and more abstract the description, the greater the distance.

Not all distancing techniques involve stylization. I will conclude this discussion with brief reference to two further techniques: the first is the mixing of positive and negative emotions. (This device was also included in the distancing devices used in psychotherapy, discussed in Chapter 4.) Comic relief in tragedies is a widely used device in classical drama. The introduction of comic scenes in an otherwise tragic drama probably reminds the audience that they are not merely reliving a distressful emotion from their own lives, but are in a theatre, where laughter is occurring. Similarly, in some classical drama, as in "romances," the plot introduces distressful events into action which is predominantly pleasurable: birth, marriage, triumph, and fulfillment. The mixing of experiences of pleasure and pain helps to keep the audience from becoming lost in any one restimulated emotion. The mixture of positive and negative emotions usually increases distance even when, paradoxically, as in romances, it decreases distance by introducing distressful events.

The most precise and subtle distancing technique used in drama involves controlling the awareness of the audience. This is a device which is used in practically all classical drama, both tragedy and comedy, and is usually absent in modern drama (except comedy, where it is still used) and in sports and game contests. In the next chapter I will discuss awareness control as a way in which the playwright includes or excludes characters in drama from the awareness the audience has about the dramatic action.

The Ritual Management of Repressed Emotion in Entertainment

Given the theory of distancing, it is possible to make some provisional judgments about the relative efficacy of the various forms of mass entertainment in the ritual management of emotions. It is not possible to evaluate precisely the extent to which the various forms of mass entertainment lead to catharsis, since there have been no systematic studies of this phenomenon. As indicated in Chapter 1, the numerous studies of the effects of TV violence contain no measure of distancing and make no distinction between the creation of distress and of catharsis.[2] In the absence of systematic studies, I will make some judgments based on my own informal observations of audiences reacting to the different forms of entertainment.

From the point of view of this theory, comedy is the contemporary form which best succeeds. In animated cartoons, farce, slapstick, situation comedy, and the stand-up routines of comedians, the distressful subject matter (such as aggression and public mistakes) is sufficiently distanced so that collective laughter occurs. Furthermore, when comedy does fail, it usually fails because of over- rather than underdistancing. Since overdistanced entertainment is never financially profitable, surviving comedies are those that are optimally distanced. It is difficult even to conceive of underdistanced comedies. Perhaps some of Pinter's plays overwhelm audiences with restimulated embarrassment or anger to the point where there is little laughter, but these are rare exceptions.

In the case of the various types of dramas based on fear, however, almost all of the entertainment available to the public is underdistanced. The dramas of suspense, terror, horror, disaster, and violence which are commercially successful certainly evoke fear or anxiety (and in some cases, anger) in most members of the audience, but seldom produce the shivering and sweating that is the sign of the

2. As suggested in Chapter I, it is possible that the distancing paradigm can be used to resolve some of the conflicting findings in the study of the effects of television violence. One of the earliest studies, by Feshback and Singer, reported that boys who watched TV violence showed *less* aggression than boys in the control group (those who watched nonviolent TV fare). More recent studies consistently report the opposite finding: children exposed to violence on TV show more aggression than those who are not (Geen, 1976). From reading the list of programs (p. 57) which Feshback and Singer's subjects watched, I would guess that those programs were more distanced and contained less violence than more recent TV fare. Some of the more distanced programs on the Feshback and Singer list were: *Batman, Get Smart, Hercules, I Spy, Superman, Tarzan,* and *Zorro.* These programs used one or more of the distancing techniques discussed above.

catharsis of fear. The audiences I have observed seem to experience the still, bone-dry fear which is indicative of distress rather than catharsis. Some viewers of these types of dramas complain of being more, rather than less, tense at the end of the drama. A recent article reports several psychiatric casualties produced by viewing the film *The Exorcist* (Bozzuto, 1975). The problem with these films seems to be that audiences become so involved that they experience the dramatic action as if it were happening to them. Under these conditions, the fear that is restimulated is so overwhelming that no catharsis takes place.

There are several dramas which may be partial exceptions to this criticism. Films like *Sugarland Express, Jaws,* and *Carrie,* in which the evocation of fear is mixed with laughter, may be sufficiently distanced to allow the catharsis of fear, as well as anger and/or embarrassment. In these films, however, fear predominates over laughter. For this reason, they are still quite underdistanced, even though less so than most fear dramas. Perhaps a better approach to the catharsis of fear would be forms in which there is a mixture of shivering and laughter, but with laughter predominating. This mixture occurs in children's entertainments like the telling of ghost stories, and the thrill of roller coaster rides. The only dramatic forms that approximate this mixture are what I would call the monster comedies, such as the Abbott and Costello series, with *Abbot and Costello Meet Frankenstein* being a representative title. These films were unusual in that they featured an adult male (Costello) as being almost continually frightened, in a comic context. Comedy-suspense forms, like *Arsenic and Old Lace,* probably would not fit into this same category as well, since the evocation of fear is minimal and/or overdistanced.

The device of increasing distance by mixing laughter

with fear, grief, or anger was discussed above. Most fear dramas, however, appear to be quite underdistanced. Viewers may leave the experience with feelings of restlessness, tension, or headaches, or have bad dreams afterwards. Children in Himmelweit's study reported having bad dreams after viewing detective dramas on television (1958, 200), which may be a sign of an underdistanced experience of repressed emotion.

The daytime serials, love stories, game shows, and sports contests fall somewhere between the two extremes in the amount of distancing and discharge. Daytime serials probably do lead to occasional crying, but it is not clear how extensive and widespread the crying is. Furthermore, the crying that does occur may be somewhat underdistanced, resulting in feelings of hopelessness or tension, rather than relief. The treatment of distressing events at an optimal distance, as in the way that death is handled in *Zita, Lies My Father Told Me,* and *Cousin, Cousine,* is relatively rare.

Game shows and sports contests allow for some catharsis of embarrassment and possibly anger, particularly for viewers of live events. At live contests, emotional contagion and the opportunity that spectators have for shouting, laughing, and energetic movement leads to some catharsis. Still, live contests do not result in optimal distancing for most of the viewers. The Hall distance is relatively great, and there is little use of stylization. (Football and hockey are partial exceptions. Helmets and faceguards may act as masks, to some extent, decreasing identification with the players.) Perhaps one of the chief failings of live contests in terms of distancing is the lack of awareness control. Players and audience share awareness, by and large, in live contests. (The one exception that comes to mind is the "instant replay." There is discrepant awareness here, but it is so brief that it probably has little effect on distancing.) There is, therefore, little opportunity to modulate identification. This is true even in professional wrestling, where there is usually a hero and a villain.

Conclusion

This chapter has presented a theory of ritual and mass entertainment as the distanced reenactment of situations which evoke collectively held emotional distress. Since the theory distinguishes between under-, over-, and aesthetically distanced ritual, it integrated the positive and negative orientations toward ritual in social science. Effective ritual is the solution to a seemingly insoluble problem, the management of collectively held, otherwise unmanageable distress. Ritual is unique in that it has the potential, at least, of meeting individual and collective needs simultaneously, allowing individuals to discharge accumulated distress and creating social solidarity in the process.

Although effective rituals are rare in modern societies, they are not completely absent. One notable instance is the success of the Chinese Communists in creating social forms which allow cathartic release. One such form is guerrilla theatre (Hinton 1966, 314–315):

As the tragedy of [a] poor peasant's family unfolded, the women around me wept openly and unashamedly. On every side as I turned to look tears were coursing down their faces. No one sobbed, no one cried out but all wept together in silence. The agony on the stage seemed to have unlocked a thousand painful memories, a bottomless reservoir of suffering that no one could control . . . the women, huddled one against the other in their dark padded jackets, shuddered as if stirred by a gust of wind. . . . abruptly the music stopped, the silence on the stage was broken only by the chirping of a cricket. At that moment I became aware of a new quality in the reaction of the audience. Men were weeping, and I along with them.

Another form was the "Speak Bitterness" meeting (Belden 1949, 487–488): "People confessed, not their sins, but their sorrows. This had the effect of creating emotional solidarity. For when people poured out their sorrows to each other, they realized they were all together on the same sad voyage through life, and from recognition of this they drew closer to one another, achieved common sentiments, took sustenance and hope." It could be argued that these contemporary ritual forms were a necessary part of the Chinese Communist revolution in that they met individual and collective needs at the same time. Mass catharsis may have been necessary to remove the apathy and paralysis of the peasants, on the one hand. On the other, the group catharsis created the conditions for solidarity and trust which were needed to insure the Communist victory.

In the modern world, even among the devout, religious observances—marriage ceremonies, funeral rites, and other surviving rituals—do not usually occasion this kind of restorative catharsis. I would like to speculate on the reasons that modern ritual has lost its effectiveness.

The phenomenon of distancing, which is the key feature of the theory proposed here, points to an important problem with ritual in the modern context. Most surviving ritual increases distance from distress: in prayer, one assumes one is conversing with a supernatural benefactor; the belief in an afterlife assures one that the dead are not lost forever; in the ritual of parting, one uses a language which intimates that the separation is temporary. These ritual forms, it seems to me, are remainders from historical eras in which ritual was needed as a protection from underdistancing. Daily life involved a succession of distressful encounters: the danger of attack from predators, whether animal or human; the risk of disease, fire, or famine; the frustration or embarrassment of rank injustice or insult.

In modern societies, however, the occasions for overt distress are fewer: civil order usually guarantees freedom from flagrant attack or abuse. Rampant danger from disease, fire, or famine has been brought under control, at least in Western societies. The occasions for distress that exist are more hidden and subtle. Even in a funeral, where one is presumably brought in contact with death, modern practice often hides, rather than reveals, the fact of death.

In this context, the kind of ritual that is needed may be one which evokes less, rather than more, distance from distress. The Chinese Communist guerrilla theatre again provides an instance. The centuries of suffering of the peasants, which was at first taken for granted and unacknowledged by the new regime, was evoked in the theatre by reenactments of the suffering of a typical family under the old regime. These realistic dramas of oppression elicited mass weeping, as indicated in the earlier quotation. It is possible that a large segment of the mass media audience in the United States is currently fascinated with violence, horror, and disaster drama because it represents an unconscious search for experiences which decrease distance so that catharsis might occur. Perhaps the key to the effectiveness of ritual is that there are two different types of distancing devices—those that increase distance and those that decrease it. For occasions in which the members of a community are overdistanced from emotion, which is the predominating case in modern societies, a ritual which decreases distance by evoking past scenes of collective distress is required.

This chapter has also applied a theory of the distancing of emotion to the problem of conceptualizing the impact of mass entertainment on viewers. Four different kinds of mass entertainments were considered: romantic tragedy, fear dramas, contests, and comedy. In keeping with the theoretical framework, each of the four forms is discussed in terms of its efficacy in the ritual management of repressed emotion; comedy is suggested to be the most successful, fear dramas the least, and contests and romantic tragedy falling between the two extremes.

These judgments are quite provisional, for two reasons. First, I made judgments on the basis of my own unsystematic observations of the reactions of audiences to entertainments I had myself viewed. Systematic observation might lead to very different results. Second, and more fundamental, the theoretical framework on which these arguments are based is itself untested. The evidence I have presented here in support of the theory is at best fragmentary and is, for the most part, illustrative rather than systematic evidence. More direct tests of the theory are found in Chapter 7.

Even without complete proof, producers of ritual mass entertainment might want to explore some of the implications of this analysis. Perhaps the most immediate problem lies in fear-anger forms: dramas of suspense, terror, disaster, and violence. I have suggested that these are the most underdistanced forms and the least effective in the ritual management of distress. It seems to me that most of these use virtually none of the distancing devices I have described: increasing the Hall distance, stylization, mixing positive with negative emotions, and discrepant awareness. I suppose that the producers are unwilling to risk increasing the distance in fear and anger dramas, since overdistancing means almost certain financial failure, and underdistanced dramas of this type often are great financial successes. To the extent that the theory proposed here is correct, however, to that extent it may be that fear dramas would attract even larger audiences if they were more optimally distanced. Although it is true that a large segment of the population is attracted by underdistanced fear dramas, it seems likely that an even larger segment of the population is repulsed by them. It seems reasonable to conclude that deliberately exploring the use of distancing devices in fear-anger dramas, toward the end of promoting more optimal distancing and catharsis, might be a profitable endeavor, as well as good public policy.

I have discussed the problem of contemporary fear-anger dramas at some length, because I see them as the least effective in the management of distressful emotion, while at the same time being the most effective in evoking emotion. I believe that the same reasoning applies to the other entertainment forms, but in lesser degree, or perhaps in a different direction. It may be, for example, that the main problem in live theatre is not increasing the distance, to protect the audience from underdistancing, but decreasing it, to discourage overdistancing.

It is conceivable that mass entertainments which could produce collective catharsis could substitute, at least in part, for the increasingly impoverished rituals in modern societies, as arenas in which a sense of community is generated. Perhaps the theatre and film, with their large community audiences, could deal with social themes that would lead to a renewal of communal bonds, and television, with its small-family viewers, could emphasize interpersonal themes, which might lead to a renewal of intimate bonds. At any rate, the theory and analysis offered here suggest a number of new directions in research and policy, as well as ideas for further debate on what seem to be important issues.

6.

A Theory of Catharsis in Drama

In the first act of *Hamlet,* when Horatio has come to tell Hamlet that he has seen what he thinks is the ghost of Hamlet's father, there is a brief moment in which first Horatio and then Hamlet misunderstand the import of what is being said. In response to a comment about his father's funeral, Hamlet says:

> My father, methinks I see my father.
> Horatio: Where, my lord?
> Hamlet: In my mind's eye, Horatio.
> . . . .
> Horatio: My lord, I think I saw him yesternight.
> Hamlet: Saw? Who?
> Horatio: My lord, the king your father.
> Hamlet: The king my father?

The audience, but not Hamlet, knows that Horatio has just seen the ghost of Hamlet's father and may understand why he starts, and the import of his question when Hamlet says "methinks I see my father." Hamlet, of course, is excluded from this understanding. Similarly, the audience can understand Hamlet's confusion when Horatio tells him that he has seen his father. Although this episode is no more than a grace note in the orchestration of the first act, it provides an example of the kind of dramatic situation which occurs almost continuously in classical and modern drama. What is the purpose of this episode? Why do we find the protagonist, Hamlet, momentarily confused and oblivious at the beginning of this play? I will argue that the construction of this episode, and the many similar episodes in this and other plays, is of crucial importance for the understanding of the dynamics of audience response. In the last part of this chapter, I will explain the significance of this episode, as part of an analysis of the relationship between the structure of the play and the movement of audience response.

My thesis concerns the playwright's use of audience awareness and identification with the characters to bring on catharsis: a theory of catharsis will help us to understand the structure of many, or perhaps even most, classical dramas. First, I will briefly discuss catharsis. Second, I will outline the relationship between certain aspects of a play's structure, particularly the kinds of awareness it generates in the audience, and catharsis. Finally, for the purpose of illustration, I will apply these ideas to the detailed analysis of the play with which this chapter started, *Hamlet*.

The earliest reference to catharsis is found in Aristotle, as indicated in Chapter 1. In the *Poetics*, he proposed that the purpose of tragedy is to purge the audience of pity and terror. He believed that catharsis had extremely important consequences for the audience, as individuals, and as members of a community. His discussion is brief and cryptic, however. He does not define catharsis nor does he describe very clearly the conditions under which it takes place and the specific consequences it may have.

There are two traditions of literary criticism that are relevant to my analysis here. The first concerns the analysis of drama from the point of view of its effects on audience response. Harbage (1947), for example, focuses on the devices Shakespeare used to promote certain effects on the audience: "My central idea is that Shakespeare's plays are designed to stimulate but not to disturb, to provide at once pleasurable excitement and pleasurable reassurance."

Harbage's idea of the combination of excitement and reassurance is quite parallel with my definition of optimum distancing, the balance between distress and safety, between participation and observation. A more recent analysis of the ways in which the design of drama creates effects on audiences can be found in Honigmann (1976).

The second tradition concerns the genesis of drama out of ritual, particularly rituals of celebration. Holloway (1961) makes the comparison between drama and myth and ritual: "The great imaginative work [of drama] . . . like the myth seems to be a source of power, of sustained, renewed or enhanced vitality, in the life of the community or individual, and it proves to exercise this power through effects, as Johnson reminded us, which are outstandingly moving and agitating. Certainly, the same may be said of some of the major rituals of any society. . . ."

Barber (1959) makes a similar comparison, and also connects ritual with catharsis, as I have in Chapter 5: "A saturnalian attitude, assumed by a clear-cut gesture toward liberty, brings mirth, an accession of wanton vitality. In the terms of Freud's analysis of wit, the energy normally occupied in maintaining inhibition is freed for celebration." These discussions are on the same track as my analysis here, but they leave the psychological sources and effects of emotional expression implicit.

In his analysis of the psychological response to drama, Freud is somewhat more explicit. He argues that dramatic scenes move audiences because they touch upon repressed emotion (Holland, 1964, 33). The scenes need not be exactly equivalent to the actual historical experiences of the members of the audience. There are certain human experiences, Freud thought, which are universal. Scenes of separation and loss can be expected to restimulate repressed grief, just as scenes depicting danger to life will resonate with the repressed fear in most members of the audience. In Freud's analysis, however, catharsis is not specifically defined, nor is there explicit discussion of the mechanisms of discharge. I will next apply the theory of catharsis and distancing outlined in Chapter 3 to the analysis of the structure of classical drama.

The purpose of this chapter is not to demonstrate that the theory of catharsis is true, but rather to suggest that this theory may be useful for understanding dramatic structures, even for those who do not believe the theory. I will seek to show that classical plays are constructed as if their authors believed the theory. This is not to suggest that the playwrights actually held such conscious beliefs. The playwrights' use of the principles of the theory was probably entirely intuitive. Shakespeare was an actor; he undoubtedly saw with his own eyes the kinds of constructions that moved audiences. I am suggesting that it would be helpful to recognize that an implicit theory of catharsis seems to underlie the structure of classical drama, even if the theory itself turns out to be untrue.

Not all dramas are constructed so as to lead the audience to catharsis. In relation to the theory, dramas can be divided into three types. In the first, emotional response is minimized. These are the dramas of ideas, which appear to be aimed at provoking an intellectual rather than an emotional response, such as some of Shaw's plays. Plays which are designed to provide information, or political propaganda, such as in socialist realism, also belong in this group. Since the appeal of these dramas is largely intellectual, they can be called the Apollonian type. From the aesthetic point of view, they would be said to be over-distanced from emotion.

At the opposite extreme, there is the second type of drama, which provokes the most violent and intense emotional reaction in the audience. In classical Roman drama, the plays of Seneca are representative. Contemporary examples of the type are dramas of suspense and horror, such as the Grand Guignol, the detective story, and all dramas of cruelty and violence. The effect of these is to provoke strong feelings without resolution, leaving the audience stranded, therefore, at the end with feelings of anxiety, fear, and grief. Such dramas lead the audience to an emotional response, but it is emotional distress, rather than discharge. In terms of aesthetic theory, these dramas are underdistanced from emotion.

The third type of drama is oriented toward catharsis, seeking neither pure thought without emotion, as in the first, or naked emotion without any thought, as in the second, but a balance between thought and feeling. Much of classical and modern drama seems to be of this type. It is represented strongly in the works of playwrights of all periods — Sophocles, Shakespeare, Jonson, Goldsmith, Sheridan, Ibsen, and Wilde — and in many of the works of today's popular culture — "situation comedies" on television and daytime serials on the radio. These dramas seek aesthetic distance from emotion, neither too far nor too close.

These three types of dramas correspond to three basic orientations toward emotion which pervade the institutions of an entire society. The Apollonian type represents that tendency in society which seeks to suppress emotion, not only in drama, but in all other institutional spheres: family, school, work, and so on. Emotion is equated with irrationality and disorder. In our present society, this orientation appears to predominate.

The Dionysian type corresponds to the opposite extreme, an orientation which seeks a sensationalism of emotional experience. The exploitation of violence, drugs, and sex which occurs in our society is evidence of this orientation. Although this approach appears to be much weaker in our society than the Apollonian, it is strongly represented in some institutional spheres; e.g., in the mass media, as the enormous commercial success of the current terror and horror films suggests.

Finally, the orientation toward catharsis, which depends on balance between thought and feeling, is only slightly represented in modern social institutions. Although this orientation seems to have been central in most of the rituals and ceremonies of preliterate and classical societies (as in the theatre in Athenian democracy), it appears to be the weakest of the three in present-day industrial societies. It is represented most strongly in drama and the arts, popular music, in some forms of psychotherapy and the human-potential movement, and, to a rapidly decreasing extent, fundamentalist religions.

Like other social forms, drama tends to reflect the pervasive influences in a society. In contemporary drama, the cathartic type faces strong competition from the other two types. Of the three types of drama, the theory of catharsis is relevant to an understanding of the construction of only the third type. The other two types are designed differently to attain different ends. In the remainder of this chapter, discussion will be limited to the cathartic type of drama. Since almost all of Shakespeare's plays appear to be oriented toward catharsis, most of the examples will be taken from his plays, although many contemporary film, television, or radio dramas would serve equally well.

Identification and Awareness in the Audience

Suppose a playwright wished to create a play that would give the audience ample opportunity for discharge of distressful emotion, how would he use the theory outlined here? The theory suggests that he is faced with two major tasks: *first,* providing scenes which touch upon the repressed emotions that are shared by most members of the audience and, *second,* constructing the scenes in such a way that the audience is sufficiently involved so that they can feel the repressed emotions, but not so involved that they are overwhelmed by them. In terms of the theory, the play must create conditions which lead to the restimulation of repressed emotion in the audience, under a balance of attention, allowing them to be both participants in, and observers of, the dramatic scenes.

For the first task, creating scenes which touch upon collective emotion, the theory is useful in only a very general way. It specifies the four basic distressful emotions as grief, fear, embarrassment, and anger, which suggests the need for scenes of loss and separation (to touch upon repressed grief), danger to life and limb (for fear), shame and humiliation (to provoke embarrassment), and scenes depicting injustice or frustration (to arouse anger). The theory is not any more specific than this: to be successful in arousing repressed emotion, the playwright must be in touch with the particular emotional idiom of his culture and milieu, perhaps drawing on his intuitive knowledge of his own emotions.

For the second task, creating a balance of attention, the theory is much more specific. It suggests the need for controlled identification of the audience with the major characters, identification that is sufficiently intense so that the audience participates with the characters in the emotion-arousing scenes vicariously, but not so intense that the members of the audience forget where they are, relive the distressful experiences, and are unable to discharge. There are a number of ways that playwrights obtain identification with their characters, some obvious, others not so obvious.

One conventional way of getting audience identification with a character is by making him or her an embodiment of the ideal values of the audience. The hero or heroine who is physically attractive, courageous, and intelligent will be identified with by the audience, to the extent that it holds these values. A second tactic is the use of characters who are similar to the members of the audience. For an audience of children, child characters, for an audience of men, male characters, and so on. Although both of these tactics are useful, they have severe limitations. There is some conflict between the first and the second, since if a character is clearly to be an embodiment of ideal values, he or she may seem stilted and artificial, too unlike the members of the audience, and not be identified with. On the other hand, if the characters are too much like the members of the audience, the audience may find them to be lusterless and will again fail to identify with them. Furthermore, the use of ideal values and of similarity to create identification is selective of possible audiences. Since audiences differ in composition and in what they value, dramas will lack universal appeal unless they use devices in addition to value and similarity to create identification.

There is one dramatic device for creating identification between audience and characters which has universal applicability, since it is based upon processes that occur in all human interaction. The device may be termed awareness control, and the universal human processes on which it is based are the processes of social inclusion and exclusion. The sharing of private information between members of a group promotes a strong, primitive sense of inclusion— of belonging and therefore of identification—between the members, just as the withholding of this information creates a strong sense of exclusion among those from whom the information is withheld.

The pressure toward identification is probably strongest, almost irresistible, when inclusion and exclusion are occurring simultaneously and visibly for the persons who are being included. The sight of others being excluded, as he is being included, seems to heighten the included person's sense of belonging to and identifying with the group. But this is exactly the situation that occurs almost continuously in dramas of the cathartic type, with the audience being included in shared awareness with one or more of the characters, while one or more of the other characters are being excluded. The effects of this device are subtle but extraordinarily powerful.

Some of the effects of awareness control have been noted in dramatic criticism. Wayne Booth (1961) has made an extensive contribution with his study of the technique he calls "sympathy through the use of inside views." His work in this area can be illustrated by a passage from his analysis of Jane Austen's novel *Emma:*

By showing most of the story through Emma's eyes, the author insures that we shall travel with Emma rather than stand against her. It is not simply that Emma provides, in the unimpeachable evidence of her own conscience, proof that she has many redeeming qualities that do not appear on the surface; such evidence could be given with authorial commentary, though perhaps not with such force and conviction. Much more important, the sustained inside view leads the reader to hope for good fortune for the character with whom he travels, quite independently of the qualities revealed (245–246).

This passage implies, quite correctly, I think, that the more one shares awareness with another, other things being equal, the more one identifies with the other. This holds true both in the sense of sympathy, which Booth stresses, and also in the sense that is more important here, of more readily taking the point of view of another, of seeing things, if only momentarily, from someone else's vantage point. The proviso "quite independently of the qualities revealed," at the end of the passage by Booth, is quite important for our purposes, since it suggests that shared awareness encourages identification, *independently* of ideal values and of likeness. As we shall see in the discussion of villains below, this device allows the play to produce some identification with all the major characters, including those who are utterly unlike and whose values are despicable to the members of the audience.

This is not to say that shared awareness can overrule or replace other sources of identification. It offers the playwright a device independent of the plot line and the characteristics of the audience, with which he can increase or decrease audience identification with characters who are likely to attract too little identification (villains, for example) and decrease, through exclusion, identification with characters who are likely to receive too much (tragic heroes, for example) so that the audience will not lose the balance of attention.

In other dramatic criticism, virtually all discussions of the concept of "dramatic irony" involve some acknowledgement of the effects of awareness control, albeit, in most cases, quite indirectly. Some critics see awareness control as tawdry and mechanical: *"Manufacture a misunderstanding and let the audience in on it* is a cheap but infallible recipe for making a play"* (Goddard, 1951, 27). A more appreciative position is taken by Bertrand Evans

(1960), who has used the concept of discrepant awareness as the focal point for his analysis of Shakespeare's comedies and romances. Like me, he sees awareness control as one of the fundamental bases of the appeal and power of drama.

The link between awareness control and catharsis, however, is missing from prior discussions of audience awareness. The basic point I wish to make here is that control of the amount and kind of awareness that the audience shares with each of the characters provides the playwright with a finely graded means of assuring balance of attention in the audience, and therefore the best possible chance for catharsis. For those characters who undergo distressful experiences similar to those which have occurred to members of the audience, control of the degree of shared awareness can produce partial identification, where the audience takes the role of the character, yet is conscious of its own point of view at the same time. With respect to these characters in these scenes, the audience can achieve a balance of attention.

There is a slightly different way of considering the balance of attention which is quite applicable to dramatic situations. In an area of emotional distress, if one's attention is equally divided between two contradictory viewpoints, emotional discharge is likely to occur. As already indicated in Chapter 5, this conception corresponds closely to Koestler's theory of laughter in *The Act of Creation* (1964). According to Koestler, we laugh at a pun because it surprises us with two contradictory meanings of a word. Ordinarily, he says, we are virtually enslaved to each of the separate meanings of the word and unaware of the conflict. The pun or joke is a situation which brings the conflict to awareness, and, for a moment, we are liberated from blind adherence to arbitrary meanings through discharge, that is, laughter. As in the present theory, Koestler believes that laughing and crying remove the blocks to creativity.

For an example of this effect, I will use a scene in Shakespeare's *The Merry Wives of Windsor* where Ford returns to his house the second time, certain he will catch Falstaff with his wife. The first time, Falstaff escaped in a basket of laundry. This time, he has disguised himself as a woman. At the moment when Ford comes to the door, his wife sends her servants out the door with the laundry basket. The audience knows that Falstaff is not in the basket. The audience also knows, however, that Ford will think that Falstaff is in the basket. Ford asks the servants what is in the basket. They reply that it is laundry. In one performance I saw, when Ford shouts for them to put down the basket, the audience roared with laughter. They continued to laugh as Ford threw item after item out of the basket. In our analysis, we would say that laughter occurs because the attention of the audience is nicely balanced between two exactly contradictory expectations. They know that Falstaff is not in the basket, but they identify partially with Ford, who has every right to expect Falstaff to be in the basket. Identifying (partially) with a character caught in an embarrassing situation, the audience discharges some of the embarrassment from earlier embarrassing episodes in their own lives through laughter, since there is a balance of attention.

The connection between awareness control and catharsis for an entire drama can be seen by briefly examining the plot of a simple comedy such as Shakespeare's *The Comedy of Errors*. The plot of this play, like many comedies, is based solely on mistaken identities, in this case between twin brothers and between their twin servants. There is a series of misunderstandings by parents, friends, lovers, and servants. Audiences usually laugh as each of the misunderstandings occurs, because, unlike the characters, they know the source of the confusion. Suppose, however, that for a naive audience, the play was produced without the introductory passage which explains that there are two sets of twins. The production would probably result in no laughter at all. The audience would be as confused as the characters by the misunderstandings. The play, shorn only of one bit of inside information, would unfold in a silent theatre.

In *The Comedy of Errors,* awareness control is based solely on coincidence, the identical appearances of twins. In other plays, many additional devices are used, such as asides and soliloquies, disguises and other forms of misrepresentation (such as lying), and the practice of having characters or the audience eavesdrop on others. A further device is a character's supposed use of supernatural power. Oberon, in *A Midsummer Night's Dream,* and Prospero in *The Tempest,* who employ magic, are represented as invisible to other characters, but not to the audience, creating awareness control.

The Disposition of Awareness in Drama

In order to understand the fine structure of the link between awareness control and catharsis, it is necessary to categorize the degree to which the audience shares awareness with a character in a precise way. The starting place for this task is Evans' (1960) discussion of discrepant awareness and the "stairstep of awareness."

Discrepant awareness is the basic concept which Evans uses in his analysis. The scene from *The Merry Wives* discussed above provides an example of its application. Ford's awareness is discrepant with respect to the audience, since the audience knows something that he doesn't know, that Falstaff is not in the basket. For Evans, discrepant awareness is a fundamental principle of Shakespearean, and, indeed, all classical drama.

Although Evans' analysis is certainly helpful, there are two difficulties with the concept of discrepant awareness as an analytic tool. In the first place, the concept deals only with the process of social exclusion (of characters from whom information known to the audience is withheld), which is only one side of awareness control. The other side is the process of social inclusion of the characters with whom the audience shares information. The concept of awareness control subsumes both processes and is therefore more general.

In the second place, a terminology is needed which stresses the asymmetry of awareness structures between audience and characters in cathartic dramas. The discrepancy of awareness in such dramas is almost always on the part of a character, rather than the audience. It is extremely unusual for a character in these dramas to know something important that the audience doesn't know. This is the typical murder mystery format, where one character, the murderer, knows a central fact that is unknown to the audience until the end of the drama. As will be indicated below, this structure is characteristic of Dionysian dramas. In cathartic dramas, however, it is almost always the case that it is the audience which knows things that at least some of the characters don't. (A rare exception is Helena in *All's Well That Ends Well*.) For this reason it seems preferable to describe awareness structures in terms of levels of awareness. In this usage the symmetry or asymmetry of awareness structures is readily apparent. In cathartic drama the awareness level of the audience will usually be higher than that of at least one of the characters.

It is typical of Dionysian dramas for the awareness level of the audience to be below one or more of the characters.

It is not only the extreme nature of the events—murder, rape, incest—which occur in these dramas that overwhelms the audience; the awareness structure also contributes to this effect. It is possible to construct dramas in which nothing extreme actually happens but which, because of the awareness structures generated, leave the audience in a state of emotional distress. Think, for example, of some of the plays of Harold Pinter.

In cathartic drama, with the audience usually knowing more than the characters, the effects of even the most distressing events are moderated because of audience foreknowledge. Advance knowledge of a distressful event mobilizes the emotions before the event actually occurs, when it is not yet overwhelming, so that discharge can take place. By the time the event takes place, its effects have been softened by the prior discharge, so that the actual event itself is not overwhelming. It is probably for this reason that the more familiar an audience is with a play, the more effective is the play in producing catharsis. Since virtually any episode in the drama becomes emblematic of the whole, discharge can start during the opening scene. In my own case, I may begin to cry in *King Lear* when Cordelia walks onto the stage in the first act.

In Dionysian drama there is no foreknowledge, since the awareness level of the audience is lower than, or at least no higher than, that of most of the characters. When a distressing event occurs, its emotional effect is augmented by surprise. These dramas are like real life, where one rarely knows ahead of time when a distressful event will occur. As in real life, these events lead to a state of shock, rather than catharsis.

Another concept of Evans' offers a good starting place for further analysis: the stairstep of awareness. Evans notes that in most of Shakespeare's plays the characters stand in varying degrees of awareness with respect to the audience. At the bottom of the stairs are persons who, as he says, are "oblivious." These are characters who have very little understanding of what is taking place around them. A clear example is Bottom in *Midsummer Night's Dream*. He is not only unaware of the magical practices of Oberon and Puck—he is even oblivious to the meaning of the words he himself uses: "We will meet, and there we may rehearse most obscenely and courageously." Since Bottom is not aware of his mistake, but the audience is, his level of awareness in this instance is lower than that of the audience.

Shakespeare's plays contain a host of oblivious characters, e.g., Bottom, Malvolio, and Andrew Aguecheek in *Twelfth Night*, Lancelot in *The Merchant of Venice*, Dogberry in *Much Ado About Nothing*, and Elbow in *Measure for Measure*. In the comedies and romances, at least, oblivious characters are usually the comic butts. In the tragedies and histories this is not the case. Lear, for example, is not aware of the disguises of Kent and Edgar and the plans of Goneril and Regan, although the audience is. Similarly, Othello does not share the awareness of the audience of Iago's practices until the end of the play. Lear is also oblivious in another sense during much of the play, in his madness.

The examples of Lear, in tragedy, and Bottom, in comedy, suggest a kind of obliviousness which is different from that of other characters, such as Elbow, Evans, the priest in *The Merry Wives*, or Lancelot. These latter types signify, mostly in their speech, through mistakes in words (Elbow, meaning to say that he *respects* his wife, says he *suspects* her), that they are oblivious, that they don't know, and don't know they don't know, the meaning of what they are saying.

The obliviousness of Bottom and Lear, however, is of a different sort. When they speak, it is often truth, more truth than that of their more knowledgeable, or sane, companions. But they are oblivious in that, although they know the truth, they don't know they know. Perhaps we should distinguish between a low obliviousness, like that of Elbow, based on not understanding, and a high obliviousness, like that of Lear, who doesn't understand that he understands. In that case, characters like Elbow would stand at the very bottom of the awareness structure, and Lear would be higher up.

At the other end of the stair, at the top, there is usually one or more characters who share all, or nearly all, of the audience's awareness. In the comedies and romances, these characters are represented by Oberon, Portia, Rosalind, the Duke in *Measure for Measure,* and Prospero. In the tragedies and histories, representative characters are Aaron in *Titus Andronicus,* Richard III, Iago, and Edmund.

Finally, there are the characters who stand in the middle. These are persons who share awareness with the audience in some crucial matters, but who are unaware in others. For example, Claudio and Hero in *Much Ado About Nothing* practice on Beatrice and Benedick and so are at a higher level of awareness than they, but are practiced on themselves by Don John and his henchmen. In some of the plays, the structure of awareness becomes very complex, with four, five or six levels of awareness. An early (and simple) example of a multilevel awareness structure is found in one scene in *Love's Labour's Lost,* with Dumain at the bottom, overspied by Longaville, who is overspied by the King, who is overspied by Biron, who in turn is overspied by the ladies of the Princess' court.

Another type of character who probably should be placed in the middle level of awareness is one who is called "mystified" by Evans (1960). He doesn't understand, but he understands that he doesn't understand. Many of the characters in *The Comedy of Errors* are baffled by the appearance of first one and then the other twin, but they know there is something wrong, they just don't know what it is—they are not, like Elbow, oblivious.

Characters standing at the various levels of awareness recall to mind the maxim:

> He who knows not, and knows not he knows not, he is a fool. Shun him.
> He who knows not, and knows that he knows not, he is simple. Teach him.
> He who knows, and knows not that he knows, he is asleep. Waken him.
> He who knows, and knows that he knows, is wise. Follow him.

This maxim refers to four different types of awareness. For the analysis of awareness control, it will be helpful to have a single continuum of awareness which utilizes these types as well as those proposed by Evans. In addition, we will use the categories proposed by Glaser and Strauss (1964), in their analysis of the possible disposition of awareness between a nurse and a dying patient. Although their categories are based on observations in a real hospital, rather than drama, they are equally applicable, just as most of the analysis of drama in this essay is applicable to life outside the theatre.

If both the nurse and patient are aware that the patient is dying, and both acknowledge this awareness, the situation is referred to as one of "open awareness." If both are aware, but neither acknowledges his awareness, the situation is referred to as one of "pretense." If one is aware, but not the other, the situation is called "closed awareness." Finally, if one is aware and the other not, but suspects, the situation is referred to as one of a "suspicion awareness context." Glaser and Strauss's typology deals with shared and discrepant awareness in a symmetric way, and also suggests two contexts additional to Evans — suspicion and pretense.

We can now combine all of the categories discussed so far into a single scale, which will contain six steps:

Knowing that you know	{ 1. Open 2. Pretense
Knowing that you don't know	{ 3. Suspicion 4. Mystification
Not knowing that you know	5. Oblivion (High)
Not knowing that you don't know	6. Oblivion (Low)

At the lowest step (level 6) is the character who doesn't know that he doesn't know, for example, Polonius in *Hamlet*. A higher type of oblivion, level 5, not knowing that you know, is given rank 5. The next two steps, 3 and 4, are variations on knowing that you don't know. The lower of the two, mystification, is knowing that something is wrong but not knowing what it is, as in *The Comedy of Errors*. The next higher step, suspicion, is also knowing something is wrong but having a definite hypothesis as to what it is. As we shall see below, level 3 is characteristic of the play *Hamlet*.

The two highest steps are variations of knowing that you know. The lower of the two, pretense, is given rank 2: you know that you know, but don't acknowledge this to the other(s). The highest step is open awareness, where you know you know, and acknowledge this to the other(s). In our analysis of *Hamlet* below, we will make use of all these levels.

Evans makes the observation that in the comedies and romances, the characters at the top of the stairs of awareness are always either young women (Portia, Rosalind, and Helena in *All's Well)*, or powerful, godlike figures (Oberon, the Duke in *Measure for Measure,* and Prospero). I would add the observation that in the histories and tragedies, a third type of character appears at the top of the stairs—the arch-villain—that is, Aaron, Richard III, Iago, and Edmund. Why is it that we find such disparate types as young women, godlike figures, and villains at the top of the awareness stair?

It would be useful for understanding the dramatic effects of the structure of awareness, in fact, if we had some way of accounting for the positioning of the characters at all levels of the awareness stair, top, middle, and bottom. How does Shakespeare distribute awareness among different types of characters and situations? This is the problem which will be explored next.

As indicated above, the ideal values and composition of the audience are two bases for identification with different types of characters. If Shakespeare assumed that most of his audience would be made up of law-abiding males, he may have placed villains and heroines at the top of the stairstep of awareness to make sure that the audience did not underidentify with them. To understand the placement of the omnipotent figures at the top of the stairs, we need to refer to a third basis for identification, which is derived from the theory of catharsis—the level of distress a character experiences.

Characters who encounter virtually no distress, at least in the comedies and romances, will be found at the top of the stairs: Oberon, Prospero, and the Duke are virtually omnipotent; Portia and Rosalind, because of their wit and readiness, are never really in danger.

At the bottom of the stairs are characters oblivious to what the audience knows. Here we find two kinds of characters. In the comedies and romances, there are the fools, in the tragedies, the heroes. How can we account for the presence of these characters at the bottom of the stairs, according to the amount of distress they undergo?

The explanation for the position of the tragic heroes, such as Lear and Othello, near the bottom of the stairs, follows straightforwardly from our theory. The situation of these characters is stark and overwhelming. The playwright's problem is to control for too much identification lest the audience become overwhelmed with distress and lose the balance of attention. He therefore places them at the bottom of the stairs to minimize overidentification.

The position of fools, like Ford and Bottom, at the bottom of the stairs is somewhat puzzling. According to our theory, we would expect to find them in the middle, since they undergo moderate distress, that is, embarrassment. Perhaps the universal embarrassment of being in a social situation where you don't know, and don't know you don't know—of feeling, therefore, hopelessly isolated from others—is also overwhelming, like the distress of the tragic heroes. If this were the case, the playwright would control for overidentification by placing them at the bottom of the stair.

Persons who encounter severe but not overwhelming distresses will be found in the middle level of awareness—Claudio, Hero, Angelo, Isabella, etc. This device works as follows: With persons at the middle level, the audience's partial identification is encouraged. We share with Hero her awareness of the strategy to unite Benedick and Beatrice. However, the audience knows something that she does not know—the plot against her by Don John. The structure of awareness between Hero and the audience is complex: There is shared awareness in some situations and discrepant awareness in others. According to our theory, the result should be partial identification. The shared awareness leads to identification, but the discrepant awareness prevents the audience from becoming completely involved with her, since it maintains the audience's point of view as different from, and, therefore, separate from Hero's. This splitting of the audience's attention between involvement and detachment corresponds exactly to the concept of balance of attention and should lead, therefore, to catharsis.

Some justification for the thesis advanced here is found in the fact that in the romances, such as *Pericles, Winter's Tale,* and *Cymbeline,* where the heroines, Marina, Perdita, and Imogen are exposed to severe distressful experiences, they no longer stand at the top of the awareness stair as did their earlier counterparts, Portia, and Rosalind, but are situated now in the middle. Rosalind, Portia, Oberon, the Duke, and Prospero, who share awareness with the audience, are exposed to virtually no distress. Viola represents a transitional figure, whose environment is no longer completely safe (she is challenged to a duel by Sir Andrew and faces the humiliation of exposure by Olivia and Orsino). Therefore, she stands near, but not at the top, of the awareness stair (unlike the audience, she is not aware of the arrival of her brother Sebastian).

The argument is, therefore, that the playwright uses the structure of awareness as a device independent of the story line, to ensure the proper amount of identification between the audience and the various characters, thus providing the conditions which lead to balance of attention and the possibility of discharge of distressful emotions. This formulation seems to explain the disposition of awareness for most of the characters in the comedies and romances and for some of the characters in the tragedies and histories.

The Movement of Audience Response

As the final part of this chapter, I will apply the theory developed here to an analysis of one aspect of *Hamlet*. The analysis so far has been static; we have considered the relationship between the awareness structure and the audience response at any given time. I will now explore the movement of audience response as it is related to changes in the degree of awareness of a single character. For this purpose Lesser's discussion of audience response to tragedy will be useful. Lesser (1957, 238–268) argues that the position of the audience relative to the drama must change during the course of the tragedy. He notes that initially, in the early parts of the play, the audience begins merely as observer. As the drama unfolds, however, the audience gets drawn into the action, participating vicariously, identifying with the characters, and experiencing, therefore, the same kinds of tensions that they would if they were actually involved in the situations depicted in the play. Lesser goes on to note that in a tragedy there must also be some point before the end of a play at which the audience begins to return to the role of observer, so that it does not participate, if only vicariously, in the hero's destruction.

The ideas discussed in this chapter give us a way of evaluating how well Lesser's doctrine applies to the structure of any particular drama, in this case, *Hamlet*. The complexity, ambiguity, and the very number of awareness structures in Hamlet are intimidating. The play is a labyrinth of awareness structures. In the first place, there are an unusually large number of asides and soliloquies. Most of these are by Hamlet, but there are also a significant number by Gertrude, Polonius, and Claudius. Second, there is a considerable amount of eavesdropping, where one or more characters overspy other characters. In the beginning of the second act, like an overture,

Polonius instructs Reynaldo how to spy on Laertes. Actual eavesdropping occurs in Act II, scene i, when Claudius and Polonius overspy Hamlet and Ophelia; in scene ii, when Hamlet and Horatio covertly watch Claudius during the play-within-the-play; in scene iii, where Hamlet watches the King at prayer, Polonius eavesdrops on Hamlet and Gertrude from behind the arras, and where Hamlet and Gertrude are overspied by the ghost. In Act V, Hamlet and Horatio overspy first the gravediggers and then Claudius, Gertrude, and Laertes at Ophelia's grave, before revealing themselves.

The complexity of the eavesdropping scenes is greater than the simple stairsteps of *Love's Labour's Lost*. In the scenes where Hamlet is overspied, one senses that he is aware, or at least suspects, that he is being watched. In the graveyard scene, Hamlet and Horatio are on a higher level of awareness than the gravediggers and Claudius' party in that they are eavesdropping, but they are on a lower level in that Hamlet and Horatio do not know that Ophelia is dead and that the grave is hers, as do the other characters and the audience.

Finally, there are a large number of discrepancies in awareness based on hidden knowledge. Most of these structures are of short duration. There are two, however, which last for virtually the entire play and are of central significance. Before discussing these, I will list the lesser structures.

The longest of these is the awareness of the ghost, which figures from the beginning of the play through the end of Act III, when it appears to Hamlet, but not to Gertrude, in her chamber. Neither Claudius nor any of his party is ever aware of the ghost. A related awareness structure is the question that Hamlet raises about the ghost, whether the information it imparts is actually from his father's spirit, or a devil, or is merely a manifestation of Hamlet's imagination. This structure is interwoven with the most important awareness structure in the play, the question of how King Hamlet, Hamlet's father, died, which will be discussed below. Another of the lesser structures concerns the status of Rosencrantz and Guildenstern. The audience knows, but it is never explicitly revealed to Hamlet, that they are employed by Claudius. Hamlet is at least suspicious of them, however, from the moment of their arrival.

Another structure concerns Claudius' plot to send Hamlet to England, ostensibly as ambassador, but actually to have him put to death. Again Hamlet suspects the true purpose, but the audience knows, since Claudius has revealed it directly in a soliloquy. At the beginning of Act IV, as she promised Hamlet, Gertrude does not reveal their conversation to the King, telling him only that Hamlet is mad, creating discrepant awareness between the audience, Hamlet, and Gertrude, on the one side, and Claudius, on the other. At the end of this act, Claudius and Laertes reveal to the audience their plot to kill Hamlet.

Although all of the discrepancies in awareness listed above are important to the plot, they are all, with the exception of the awareness of the ghost, more or less incidents among many others in the unfolding action. There are two crucial structures, however, which encompass virtually the entire play. The first is the question of how King Hamlet died, the second is the nature of Hamlet's "madness." I will first discuss the structure concerning Hamlet's madness.

At the end of Act I, after his scene with the ghost, Hamlet tells Horatio and Marcellus, and thus reveals to the audience, that he will feign madness ("an antic disposition"), putting these characters and the audience on a higher step of awareness than Claudius, Polonius, Gertrude, Ophelia, and, later, Laertes. This discrepancy in awareness lasts throughout most of the play and is never completely eliminated.

Claudius and his party are variously distributed along the stairstep with respect to this issue. At the lowest level (step 6), Polonius is oblivious, not knowing and not knowing that he doesn't know, that Hamlet's madness is feigned. He is certain that Hamlet is mad for Ophelia. At a somewhat higher level (step 4) Gertrude and Ophelia are mystified, knowing that they don't know the nature of his madness. Claudius is at a still higher level, step 3, suspicious. He is doubtful from the beginning of Polonius' explanation ("How may we try it further?") and, after eavesdropping on Hamlet and Ophelia, dismisses it. ("Love? His affections do not that way tend.") He is also suspicious that Hamlet may not be mad. ("Nor what he spoke, though it lacked form a little, was not like madness.")

In the ensuing scenes, Claudius acts as if he has become certain that Hamlet is not mad, although he (Claudius) continues to speak to other characters as if he were. Hamlet also continues the pretense. For much of the later part of the play, therefore, an awareness context of mutual pretense (step 2) between Hamlet and Claudius characterizes this issue.

The most important awareness structure is carefully developed in the first act. In scene v, at the point when the ghost tells Hamlet that he (the ghost) is King Hamlet, and that he was murdered by Claudius, we may place Hamlet at level 3. On the one hand, Hamlet states that he believes what he has been told ("It is an honest ghost"). On the other hand, he states at three different points in the play the possibility that the information the ghost imparts may come from the devil, and/or from his (Hamlet's) own troubled imagination. Hamlet plans to put his suspicion of Claudius to the test by the play within the play.

Even before the ghost's disclosure, however, Hamlet has had portents indicating some awareness with respect to the King's death. At the end of Act I, scene ii, his response to Horatio's news concerning the appearance of the ghost (''Foul deeds will rise . . . '') indicates that he had already sensed that something was wrong (level 4), and his reaction to the ghost's disclosure that Claudius was the murderer (''O, my prophetic soul'') indicates, retrospectively, that Hamlet had some earlier intimation of Claudius' guilt (level 5, not knowing that he knew).

After seeing Claudius' reaction to the play within the play, Hamlet initially indicates his certainty that Claudius murdered the king (''I'll take the ghost's word for a thousand pounds''). Yet as late as Act IV, scene iv, he still may have doubts ('' . . . some craven scruple of thinking too precisely on the event . . . '').[1] Although the circumstantial evidence of Claudius' guilt mounts, there was no eyewitness, nor does Claudius ever confess; rather, he dies silent. Hamlet never reaches absolute certainty about his father's death.

This is not true of the audience, however. In Act III, scene i, Claudius intimates his guilt to the audience (''Oh heavy burden''), and in scene iii he states it explicitly: ''Oh my offense is rank . . . a brother's murder. . . . '' From the point of view of the analysis used here, this revelation is the decisive stroke in the play. It accomplishes two important purposes at once. On the one hand, it in-

---

1. The word ''event'' is usually interpreted to mean outcome, suggesting that Hamlet's hesitation is based on fear of the consequences. However, it seems to me that his use of the term ''scruple'' contradicts this interpretation, suggesting hesitation on moral rather than practical grounds.

creases the likelihood of some audience identification with Claudius, by placing him in a position of shared awareness with the audience with respect to a crucial issue, and it reveals his inner suffering. On the other hand it distances the audience from overidentification with Hamlet, by creating a slight but significant discrepancy in awareness between the audience and Hamlet. Hamlet never arrives at certainty of Claudius' guilt, but the audience does. In accordance with our earlier analysis, this discrepancy in awareness separates Hamlet's perspective from that of the audience and helps prevent, therefore, complete identification.

The construction of the stairstep of awareness with respect to King Hamlet's death is strikingly ingenious. For the character of Hamlet, it allows for his continuous growth in awareness during the course of the play, in that he moves from the oblivion of level 5 (not knowing that he knows) in Act I, to the highest levels, 2 (pretense), or 1 (knowing that he knows), by Act V. At the same time, the audience, like Hamlet, has a similar experience of growth of awareness, but it moves further and faster, going from the very lowest level, 6 (not knowing that it doesn't know), in Act I, to the very highest, 1 (knowing that it knows), in Act III.

This double movement probably accomplishes several purposes at once. In the first place, Hamlet's growth in awareness with respect to his father's death parallels, and perhaps makes manifest, his inner growth of awareness in a philosophical sense, with respect to his identity and his place in the scheme of things. Second, the double movement of Hamlet and the audience allows the audience to experience—both by observing Hamlet and vicariously, in its own right—the seeming endlessness of the long corridors of awareness and, particularly, the vast abyss that can exist between level 3, suspicion, and the higher levels.

Finally, the parallel but separate movement of Hamlet and the audience allows the first two purposes of accomplishment, while still keeping separate Hamlet's perspective from that of the audience, as indicated above.

This movement in awareness conforms with Lesser's doctrine. According to Lesser, at some point after the hero's reversal of fortunes, the audience must begin to disengage from total involvement, so that it does not participate in the hero's destruction. If one accepts the argument so far, it would seem that at the end of the third act a discrepancy of awareness is created which facilitates audience disengagement.

In the larger context of the play, Hamlet's movements along the stairstep of awareness also follow Lesser's doctrine, that in tragedy the audience begins as an observer, becomes a participant, and, before the end, becomes an observer again. In the first act, Hamlet begins at a very low level on the stairstep of awareness. The central event of this act is the appearance of the ghost, yet knowledge of this event is carefully cascaded down to Hamlet: Marcellus and Bernardo, soldiers of the watch, indicate to Horatio that they have seen the ghost before the action of the play begins, then it appears to them and to Horatio, and only then to them and to Hamlet. The irony of the scene in which Horatio comes to tell Hamlet about the ghost, with which this essay began, depends upon the audience's awareness, and Hamlet's ignorance, of Horatio's awareness of the ghost. Hamlet is the butt of this sequence, since he is oblivious. According to our analysis, Hamlet's lowly position in the awareness structure in most of the first act discourages audience identification.

At the end of Act I, however, Hamlet's position on the awareness stairstep begins to rise, when he reveals to the audience his plan to feign madness. It continues to rise with the large number of his asides and soliloquies, and his counterpractices against Polonius, Rosencrantz and Guildenstern, and Claudius. It reaches its peak in Act III, scene ii, in the scene immediately following the play-within-the-play, when he reveals to Horatio his jubilation at the success of his practice on Claudius. According to our analysis, in this part of the play (between the end of Act I and the middle of Act III), the structure of the drama has encouraged the audience to identify increasingly with the hero.

Immediately following Hamlet's triumph, however, his position in the awareness structure begins to fall. As indicated above, it is at this point that Claudius discloses his guilt to the audience, placing the audience at a slightly higher level than Hamlet. In the scene where Claudius is praying, the irony of Hamlet's decision not to kill him at prayer depends upon the audience's awareness, and Hamlet's ignorance, that Claudius is unable to pray. Finally, Hamlet is practiced on, with lethal effect, by Claudius and Laertes with the poisoned foil. Futhermore, after this point the number of practices against Hamlet outnumber his counterpractices. In his audience with Gertrude, he is overspied by Polonius and by the ghost. Of all the major characters, he learns last of Ophelia's death. As indicated in our analysis, as Hamlet's place in the stairstep of awareness falls, so should audience identification. The three phases of Hamlet's awareness level outlined here therefore follow the movement of audience involvement predicted by Lesser.

If Lesser's doctrine holds true for other plays as it seems to do for Hamlet, it would have an important implication for the idea of the balance of attention and, therefore, for the argument presented here. If the structure of the play causes the audience to begin as observer, become participant, and, finally, before the end of the play, return to the role of observer, this would guarantee that the audience would pass through a balance of attention at least twice: the first time as it leaves the role of observer, perhaps somewhere in Act II, and the second time as it returns to the observer's role. It is at these two points, perhaps in Acts II and IV, that the maximum likelihood of audience catharsis would occur.

Summary

This chapter has applied the theory of catharsis to the problem of understanding the structure of classical and modern dramas. The most important principle in the theory concerns the concept of the balance of attention. The occluded emotions of the audience, which could provide one of the bases for dramas whose appeal is universal, regardless of time or place, are touched if the audience identifies with the characters neither too little nor too much, if they are able to act as both participants and observers simultaneously. In our discussion, the balance of attention has been related to the playwright's use of audience awareness control, of using the processes of social inclusion and exclusion to prevent over- or under-identification with the major characters. This analysis was applied to Shakespearean drama in two ways. First, in a comparison between the awareness levels of many different types of characters, in several plays, and second, in an analysis of the relationship between the movement of audience response and the changing level of awareness of the protagonist over the course of a single play. These applications seem to show the usefulness of the theory of catharsis for understanding the structure of the plays that were considered.

III. Research

7.

Humor and Tension:
The Effects of Comedy

Written with Stephan C. Scheele

This chapter concerns the problem of the effect of humor: Is laughter good medicine? In lay opinion, the answer is almost a truism. Laughter is widely thought to reduce tension, clear the air, and probably be beneficial in many other ways. Norman Cousins' article in the *New England Journal of Medicine* (1974) provides a dramatic representation of popular belief, since he describes how he cured himself of what might have been an otherwise fatal illness, by taking a laughing cure. After two weeks in a hospital, with his malady still undiagnosed and getting worse, Cousins stopped taking all drugs and checked into a hotel. He started his own treatment of vitamin C and laughter: "He sent out for Marx Brothers movies. A projector was set up in the room. 'I watched *A Night at the Opera* twice. It's still funny. I watched *Animal Crackers*. I sent out for segments of old *Candid Camera* shows. . . . And every day I watched the Marx Brothers and segments of *Candid Camera,* and the hours that were pain-free got longer and longer, and the more I laughed, the better I got'" (Smith 1974, 13–14). According to Cousins' account, laughter was a central component in his cure.

In theoretical discussion and in research, however, there is split opinion. Among the proponents of laughter, Freud (1905) believed that certain kinds of laughter were tension-reducing, as did Berlyne (1971). The theory of catharsis outlined in Chapter 3 posits laughter as one form of emotional discharge. Nichols and Zax (1977, 8) also list laughter as one of the cathartic processes. Other recent proponents have been Fry (1963), Greenwald (1975), Mendel (1970), and Mindess (1971).

On the other hand, there are many approaches which question the value of laughter. In studies of humor in experimental social psychology, there is a tradition of skepticism about catharsis, created by Berkowitz's (1962) work on aggression catharsis. Among psychoanalysts, laughter is often considered to be a defensive maneuver, or a covert form of hostility (Kubie, 1970). Finally, there is a tradition in medical science of considering laughter only in connection with disease (e.g., epilepsy) or psychopathology (as in the case of hebephrenia) (Stearns, 1972).

Laughter and Tension Levels

Given this division in theoretical views, it is noteworthy that there is also a split in the research findings concerning the effect of laughter on tension levels. The studies which have used a subjective measure of effect, a mood adjective checklist (MACL) have indicated that exposure to a humorous stimulus has a relaxing effect. There have been three such studies: Dworkin and Efran (1967), Singer (1968), and Berkowitz (1970). However, those studies using objective, physiological measures have indicated the opposite effect, or no effect, that humor or laughter is arousing, or at least not relaxing. This finding has been most clearly established with heart rate (HR) as the measure of effect. There have been six studies of humor and HR: Martin (1905), Averill (1969), Fry (1969), Jones and Harris (1971), Langevin and Day (1972), and Godkewitsch (1976). These findings have been interpreted by Godkewitsch (p. 135) as contradicting Freud's idea that humor may be tension-reducing and Arnheim's (1971) "cosmic principle" that tension reduction is the source of all reward and pleasure.

Before continuing the discussion of the studies of the effect of humor on heart rate, we want to indicate that there are several studies of the effects of humor or laughter on other physiological parameters. As examples, we will briefly describe studies by Fry and Stoft, Walsh, and Podolsky. The intriguing study by Fry and Stoft (1971) has some relevance to this chapter, since they investigated the physiological effects of laughter. The measure used, however—the oxygen saturation level of the blood—is not clearly related to arousal levels. It is related, however, to the broader hypothesis that laughter is the best medicine. The question that seems to underlie Fry and Stoft's study is whether it would be possible for one to laugh oneself to death. They suggest that there are three physiological characteristics of laughter which might lead to oxygen deficiency and, therefore, to strain on the heart: energy expenditure, alterations of the respiratory pattern, and activation of the sympathetic nervous system.

Since clinical experience has suggested that other activities which show these characteristics, such as sexual intercourse, can lead to heart attacks, Fry and Stoft investigated the effects of various intensities of laughter on oxygen levels in the bloodstream. They found the results quite surprising: although different intensities of laughter, ranging from mild to explosive, result in massive expiration of the breath, increased heart rate, and substantial energy expenditure, there is no effect on the oxygen level in the blood. They show that holding one's breath causes a precipitous drop, but even sustained laughter causes no change whatever. These results suggest that laughter has anomalously positive physiological effects, compared to other energy-expending activities.

In an article entitled "Tears and Laughter," in *Today's Health* (Garrison, 1971), two studies are cited. The first is by James J. Walsh of Fordham University:

In *Laughter and Health,* published more than forty-three years ago (1928) the doctor wrote of "laboratory evidence which established that a hearty, throaty laugh momentarily compensates for either high or low blood pressure." Persons with blood pressure of 180 or above experienced—through laughter—a drop of ten or more points; those with low blood pressure, below 120, evidenced a rise of ten points or more. The author concluded that those individuals with blood pressure problems would do well to "keep laughing."

A second study, by Edward Podolsky, is also mentioned:

Dr. Podolsky fed two groups of college students the same diet for two weeks. One group he "entertained" with scientific lectures. The second group was treated to the patter and monologue of a professional comedian. To the surprise of practically no one, the group of collegians who laughed through the meal at the comedian checked in with healthier "noticeably improved digestion."

As yet we have been unable to find these two studies for verification, since the article did not give exact citations. If the paraphrasing in the *Today's Health* proves to be accurate, both studies would support the hypothesis that laughter has beneficial effects.

Returning to the heart-rate studies, how can the difference between the subjective and objective findings (HR) be explained? One possibility is that the MACL and HR scores are not tapping the same phenomenon. HR may not be a valid measure of tension. The position that Lacey and

Lacey (1974) take can be interpreted in this way. They argue that the evidence on the relationship between HR and somatic or behavioral processes is quite mixed: some studies report constant relationships, others an absence of relationship, and still others, unexplained reversals. In response, however, Obrist and his collaborators (1974) suggest that under certain conditions, such as at low levels of arousal or sympathetic influence, there are invariant relationships. Since these conditions obtain in the study of humor and laughter, we will seek the explanation elsewhere.

Another possible explanation concerns the difference in methods used in the two sets of studies. It is clear in the MACL studies that the checklists were administered before and after the exposure to the entire set of humorous stimuli. The effect measured would therefore be the net change of subjective tension level caused by the whole period of exposure. Not so with the HR studies, however. Although each study used a slightly different method, it is immediately apparent that they did not measure the net change in HR. Martin (1905) measured HR only during a short period (approximately ten to fifteen seconds) following exposure to each humorous stimulus. Langevin and Day (1972) obtained a mean change in HR, but only during the fifteen seconds of exposure to each cartoon. Godkewitsch (1976) used a procedure identical to Langevin and Day. Jones and Harris measured HR for only four seconds after the stimulus. Although all of the studies used a series of humorous stimuli, none examined the cumulative or net effect of the series. Fry made no measurements at all; he simply showed a chart which seemed to indicate HR elevation was associated with laughter in two cases.

At first, Averill's study (1969) would seem to use a before and after design similar to that used in the mood adjective checklist studies. Averill's study also has assumed importance in that it is the only one of the nine studies which used both subjective and objective measures of effect. However, a close inspection shows that his study also did not measure net change. His before measurement is appropriate, since it is the mean rate for six minutes before exposure to the comic film. However, his after measurement, which should have been taken during the corresponding six minutes after the film was over, was instead taken during the last six minutes. Since he states that 78 percent of the subjects included one or more scenes from the last six minutes among the funniest in the film, it is quite likely that laughter occurred during the measurement period. Averill's procedure seems to have confounded HR change during laughter with the net change resulting from exposure to the whole film.

Given the difference between the two sets of methods, it can be seen that the HR findings and MACL findings could both be correct: during laughter or exposure to the humorous stimulus, tension increases, as indicated by elevated heart rates, but the net effect of a period of laughter or exposure is relaxation, as indicated by the MACL studies. How is it possible that HR could be elevated by each laugh, but that the net effect of a number of laughs would be to decrease HR? Perhaps after each laugh ends, HR not only returns to baseline, but overshoots, leading to a decrease in HR for a period of time. If a small amount of this decrement cumulated with each succeeding laugh, a gradual decrease in HR over the entire period of laughter would occur, which would result in the net decrease reported above.

The pattern of momentary elevation (1972) followed by a decrease is congruent with Berlyne's "arousal-jag" hypothesis: an event which initially raises arousal may be pleasurable if it is followed by a prompt reduction of arousal. It is also congruent with Gellhorn's (1963) model of the "tuning" of the autonomic nervous system: at optimum levels of activation, the firing of the sympathetic nervous system (SNS) is followed immediately by rebound firing of the parasympathetic system, which in turn is followed by a rebound of the SNS, and so on, in sequence, until the autonomic nervous system is exactly in balance. Finally, this pattern also would support the senior author's model of the discharge of emotional distress at optimal distance. This model proposes that catharsis takes place when there is an exact balance between emotional distress on the one hand, and a feeling of complete security, on the other.

The exact balance between distress and safety may appear to the individual as the simultaneous experience of participation in, and observation of, his or her own distress. The seeming simultaneity of these two disparate experiences is, however, probably only apparent. Rather, the balance between distress and discharge would be a product of an alternation between the two states that is so rapid that the two states would be experienced as fused into one. (See Chapter 3, p. 62.) This model is compatible with Gellhorn's model.

We would therefore hypothesize the net effect of a period of laughter to be a decrease in heart rate, as well as subjective feelings of tension. In order to test this hypothesis, we designed the present study to be different from earlier studies, in that it is concerned with the net effect of a period of laughter on both mood scores and heart rate.

A second difference between the present study and earlier studies concerns the difference between the effects of laughter, on the one hand, and the effects of exposure to a humorous stimulus, on the other. All of the earlier studies in this area which were available to us have involved the effects of exposure to stimuli such as cartoons, jokes, or comic films.

The practice of using exposure to humorous stimuli as

the independent variable gives rise to two issues which require discussion. The first, and more troublesome, issue is that it is difficult, without monitoring laughter, to be sure that the stimuli are actually humorous to the subjects. Let us return to the major study in this area, Averill's, once more. As already indicated, the results of this study are uninterpretable, because of the confounding of momentary and net effects. But even if these effects had been measured correctly, there would be another ambiguity in Averill's findings.

Is the lack of any significant change in HR in the comedy condition (as compared with the control condition) because humor does not affect HR or because the subjects did not find the comic film humorous? One must raise this question because Averill reports, in passing, that only eleven of the eighteen subjects in the comedy condition laughed. He does not report how much they laughed. Averill sought to resolve this issue by having the subjects rate the humor of the film they viewed. On a four point scale ("... a score of 0 indicates neutrality ... while 3 is the maximum score possible") the humorous film was rated 1.3, as against a rating of .5 for the film shown the control group, a travelogue. If one accepts humor ratings as valid, these data at least suggest that the comic film was perceived by the subjects as slightly funnier than the travelogue.

However, it seems necessary at this point to raise the question of the validity of humor or funniness ratings. Humor is probably partly an emotional response, as well as a cognitive one. It seems possible that funniness ratings may overemphasize the cognitive component of humor, at the expense of the emotional component. Ordinarily, there would seem to be something missing when the response of a person to jokes is to say "That's very funny," rather than laughing.

The available data that can be interpreted as bearing on the validity of funniness ratings, reports of the relationship between funniness ratings and laughter, is not reassuring. Singer (1968) found an intercorrelation of .74 between humor ratings and laughter. Pollio et al. (1972) found different levels of association for four different comedy routines, .01, .36, .57 and .78. The only study to center an experiment solely around this question (Branch et al., 1973) found that for the tapes of seven different comedians the correlations between the number of laughs and funniness ratings were .05, .30, .34, .51, .68, .69.

These findings suggest that, although ratings are not independent of laughter, they are also not a reliable index. Of twelve correlations, only two are large enough to account for more than half of the variance, while seven correlations are so small that they account for less than one-third of the variance. It would appear that funniness ratings usually tap aspects of humor other than its laughter potential. In addition to the question of immediate and net effects discussed above, there is a second ambiguity in Averill's findings: it is possible that the lack of significant HR changes he found is because the subjects in his study did not find the comic film they saw to be funny.

A second issue raised by the use of exposure to a humorous stimulus concerns the interpretation of causal processes. Even in those studies which show that humor reduces tension, there is no indication of the process through which this effect occurs. Humor is a very abstract concept; it might include several processes, such as the perception of and cognition about humor, as well as mirth (defined by Zigler et al. [1966] as laughter or smiling). Mirth is more specific but still does not differentiate between the effects of laughing and the effects of smiling. For this reason, it would be useful to have a study which made some attempt to differentiate between the effects of the different processes which occur as a result of exposure to a humorous stimulus—perception, cognition, smiling, or laughter.

It was proposed in Chapter 3 that spontaneous laughter (especially spontaneous laughter which occurs in response to a comedic stimulus) usually has a reflex character, standing in relationship to the tension of embarrassment (or other distressful emotion) as orgasm stands to sexual tension. Spontaneous laughter, therefore, is seen as signaling the extremely rapid resolution of tension which otherwise might have continued unabated. This tension need not be conscious or current; it could be a delayed reaction from an earlier situation or situations.

Given this approach to catharsis, it would be desirable to choose laughter, rather than exposure to a humorous stimulus, as the causal agent in a research design. Such a choice would allay the uncertainties about how humorous the stimulus was to the subjects, and it would also facilitate interpreting the causal processes involved. Tests of the catharsis hypothesis which use exposure to a humorous stimulus as the causal agent seem to us to confound the external trigger which may give rise to catharsis, with catharsis itself, an internal process, which may or may not occur.

Field Study

However, for the very reason that laughter is unpredictable, it is difficult to use it as the treatment variable in an experimental design. With a sufficiently large treatment group, one might subdivide, after the fact, into groups in which there were varying amounts of laughter—high, medium, low, and none. In this way one could differentiate between the effects of laughter and the effects of exposure to a humorous stimulus. Because the size of the treatment group available was limited, the design of the present study is a compromise: we first conducted a field study in which laughter was the independent variable and then an experiment in which exposure to a humorous stimulus was the treatment. The field study tested the hypothesis (in two different audiences) that reduction of tension, for individuals viewing a comic film, as measured by HR and by MACL scores, is positively correlated with the number of laughs reported by those individuals. In the experiment, the hypothesis is that exposure to a comedy tape will result in reduction of tension, again as measured by HR and MACL scores, as compared with a group which listens to a nonhumorous lecture. The number of laughs for each subject, as recorded by observers, and funniness ratings by the subjects, were also obtained for subsequent analysis.

Field-Study Procedure A brief questionnaire was given to two different audiences before and after viewing. From some 300 persons who viewed the film *Harold and Maude,* 243 useable questionnaires were obtained. From some 150 persons who viewed *Everything You Always Wanted to Know about Sex* (Woody Allen), 125 useable questionnaires were obtained. Both films were the same running time, about 90 minutes.

The questionnaire given before viewing contained two sections. The first concerned pulse rate; the experimenter instructed the audience how to find and count their pulse. He then asked them to count their pulse for the thirty-second interval that he timed. On the *Harold and Maude* showing, the pulse was counted only once. In the *Everything You Always Wanted . . .* showing, it was taken twice and the mean used as the measure of heart rate.

The second section of the questionnaire was a MACL,

which assessed subjective feelings of tension and relaxation. (Studies establishing the reliability of MACLs are reported by V. Nowlis [1965, 367–369].) It contained the following adjectives indicative of tension: sad, tense, withdrawn, confused, jittery, fearful, grouchy, annoyed, angry, drowsy; and the following adjectives indicative of relaxation: attentive, happy, energetic, carefree, lively, pleased, relaxed, refreshed, clear, alert. In the questionnaire, the relaxation and tension adjectives were listed alternately. After each adjective, the respondents were asked to check "Yes," "Some," or "No."

The questionnaire given after viewing was identical to the first one, with the addition of a third section questioning the amount of laughter. The question was "About how much do you think you laughed during the movie?" Viewers were asked to rate the amount from the following choices:

    (a). A lot—over thirty times;
    (b) Pretty much—fifteen to thirty times;
    (c) Some—five to fifteen times;
    (d) Hardly at all.

Change scores, based on the difference between measures before and after, were calculated for each subject. The change score for the pulse rate involved subtracting the pulse after from the pulse before. A positive change score indicated a decrease in tension. Change scores for the MACL were calculated by scoring a "yes" for the relaxation adjectives as $+2$, "some" as $+1$, and "no" as 0, and a "yes" for the tension adjectives as -2, "some" as -1, and "no" as 0. The overall change scores involved subtracting the total of the scores before from the total scores after. The larger the change score, the more relaxed the subject had become.

Field-Study Results   To test the hypothesis that the more a person laughs, the more relaxed he becomes, the joint distributions of laughter and pulse change and laughter and mood score change were calculated for the two audiences. The number of laughs were divided into these ranks: a lot, pretty much, and some or none. Mood change was ranked as low, medium, or high.

All four of the distributions are correlated in the direction predicted by the hypothesis: the more the laughter, the more the decrease in pulse and the more the decrease in subjective tension, as reflected by the MACL. Three of the four correlations (tau = .17, .19, .23) are statistically significant; one is not. (The correlation between the decrease in pulse rate and the amount of laughter for the *Harold and Maude* audience [tau = .05] is not significant at the .01 level. A possible source of error in this correlation, as compared to the other showing, is the pulse count, which was only taken once. In the other showing, it was taken twice, and the mean of the two counts was used as the pulse measure.) Although the correlations between amount of laughter and reduction of tension support the hypothesis, the support is weak because the correlations are low. Also the direction of causation is not clear because the design concerns a naturally occurring situation, rather than a controlled experiment. We therefore designed an experiment to investigate the relationship between humor and tension in a more controlled way.

Experiment

Subjects in groups of three were exposed to either experimental or control stimuli (comedy or noncomedy tapes) in a small-group laboratory. Subjects were seated so that they could be observed through a one-way mirror. They were randomly assigned to either the treatment (comedy) or control (lecture) condition. Before and after measures were MACL and HR. An after measure was taken of funniness ratings of the tape. The laughter of each subject was coded and counted by raters.

The sixty subjects were volunteers from undergraduate sociology classes. Subjects ranged from 18 to 44 in age, the mean being 20.2. Groups of three were tested in a random sequence across treatment and control conditions to avoid time or maturation effects.

Materials The comedy tape was fourteen minutes in length, containing materials from two sources. The first part consisted of four minutes by Cheech and Chong, "Let's Make a Dope Deal"; the second part, a series of sketches from the Richard Pryor album, "That Nigger's Crazy." These routines were chosen after pretesting several different tapes. The control tape, also fourteen minutes, was the introductory portion of an anthropology lecture, "Biculturalism," delivered at a midwestern college. This tape was also pretested. No occurrence of laughter was recorded.

Independent Measures The number of laughs were recorded for each subject by raters through a one-way mirror, one rater for each three subjects. The rating was blind — raters had no information regarding the experiment except for instructions as to how to code laughter. An interrater reliability check was made by randomly assigning raters to count the number of laughs by a single random subject, six times. It was found that interrater reliability was .98.

A laugh was defined as beginning when a subject showed any chest or head movement indicative of the muscle contractions associated with laughter, and the ac-

companing vocalization. The laugh was defined as ending
when any pause in such movement and vocalization could
be noticed. A funniness rating was taken after subjects listened to the tape. The rating consisted of a scale from one
to nine, with one, "Not funny at all," to nine, "Extremely
funny."

Effect Measures   The subjective measure of tension was
the same MACL used in the field study, with the exception
that each adjective was given a score from one ("not at
all") to nine ("completely") by the subjects. The scores
for the tension and relaxation adjectives were then added
for both before and after, and the difference was computed
to determine the change score. A positive score indicated
relaxation, a negative, increase in tension.

The objective measure of tension was the HR change,
accomplished by having each subject count and record his
or her pulse rate four times, successively, for fifteen seconds each, before and after listening to the tape. Southard
and Katahn (1967) found that when subjects took their own
pulse for four fifteen-second checks, the correlation between the self report and that recorded by a Grass Poly-
graph was .98, which demonstrated the accuracy of the
self-reported rates.

Procedures   Subjects in groups of three were seated in a
waiting room for eight minutes in order that an accurate
baseline heart rate could be recorded when the experiment
began. They were seated in the laboratory near the tape
recorder, facing the one-way mirror. Subjects first determined their pulse, then filled out the first MACL. The experimenter explained that they were to hear a tape, during
which he would leave the room. Afterwards, the experimenter returned, and the subjects again recorded the four

pulse rates and completed the MACL within thirty seconds of the end of the tape. Following this, they completed the funniness ratings, concluding the procedures. Raters recorded the laughter identically for both groups.

Results As can be seen in the accompanying table, the treatment tape resulted in considerable laughter, the mean number of laughs being 42.1 (with a range from 7 to 140), and the control tape, less than 1. The requirement that the treatment stimulus be perceived as much more humorous than the control stimulus seems to have been fulfilled.

Experimental and Control Comparisons

	Group 1	*Group 2*	*t value*
Mean HR before	73.7	70.7	
Mean HR after	70.7	70.4	
Mean HR change	−2.9	−0.3	−1.6
Mean MACL before†	1.2	1.7	
Mean MACL after†	1.9	1.4	
Mean MACL change**	+.6	−.2	3.6*
Mean funniness rating	6	1.6	13.3*
Mean number of laughs	42.1	0.3	8.5*

*$p < .001$
†Figures indicate mean unit distance from mean of scale (4.5)
**Figures indicate mean change toward either relaxation (+) or tension (−), expressed in units on a scale of 1 to 9.

In the treatment condition, the mean change in HR was −2.9 beats per minute, from a baseline of 73.7. The mean change in the control condition was −.3, from a baseline of 70.7. For the MACL score, the treatment condition showed relaxation, +.62 units on a 9 point scale, (p. .01) from a baseline of 1.3, while the control condition showed an increase in tension, $-.2$ units, from a baseline of 1.7. The treatment condition shows a decrease in tension on both measures, as predicted by the theory.

Analysis of Covariance

	Sum of squares	DF	F	P.
Prestimulus HR	181	1	5.0	.03
Treatment	68.8	1	1.9	.18
Explained	250			
Residual	2082			
Prestimulus MACL	6022	1	24.4	.001
Treatment	2588	1	10.5	.002
Explained	8610			
Residual	14060			

It should be noted, however, that the measure before indicates a higher level of tension in the treatment condition than in the control, even though assignment of subjects was random; mean HR in the treatment condition is three beats per minute higher than in the control, and the mean MACL score is .4 units lower (more tense). For this reason, an analysis of covariance was performed across the treatment and control conditions ($N = 60$), with membership in the treatment or control condition the main effect, and the prestimulus measures of HR and MACL score, the covariates (see accompanying table). We assume that the MACL ratings form an equal interval scale, so that the analysis will be the same for MACL scores and HR. For HR change, neither the treatment nor the prestimulus score was related at the .01 level of probability. For MACL change, both treatment and the prestimulus score were significant at the .01 level.

Rank Correlation of Number of Laughs and Funniness
Ratings with HR and MACL Score Changes,
across Treatment and Control Conditions

	Number of laughs	Funniness rating
Number of laughs		.59
HR change	−.36	.31
MACL change	−.36	.60

To determine the relationship of the number of laughs
and funniness ratings to changes in tension, the rank correlation between the three measures was calculated, across
treatment and control conditions. As indicated in the next
table, funniness rating is more highly correlated with
MACL change (r_s = .60) than laughter (r_s = .31). This
result might have been expected, since both MACL score
and funniness rating are cognitive tasks. Surprisingly,
however, the number of laughs and funniness ratings predict HR change equally well (r_s = .36). One might expect
the number of laughs, to the extent that it reflects an emotional reaction, would predict HR change better than funniness rating. This finding raises some questions about the
use of number of laughs as an index of emotional response. Perhaps amount, rather than number, of laughs
would be a better index of emotional response. That is,
observers' ratings of number, duration, and intensity of
laughs may be necessary. By intensity of laughter, we
mean the extent and strength of bodily involvement, ranging from the slight involvement of a giggle to the complete
and strong involvement of a belly laugh. It is possible that
funniness ratings are more sensitive to the amount of emotional response than the number of laughs, which is only a

mechanical count that does not discriminate between a short giggle and a lengthy belly laugh. (For a completely different approach to the relationship between laughter and funniness ratings, see Cupchik and Leventhal [1974].)

Finally, in the debriefing of subjects following the experiment, less than 10 percent of the subjects reported being aware of the hypothesis of the study.

Discussion

The results of this study with respect to effects of humor on mood are quite clear. In all three tests (the two audiences in the field study and the experiment) the findings support the hypothesis that humor lowers tension. These findings further confirm the results of the three earlier studies of the effect of humor on mood. In addition to this confirmation, the present study also suggests that laughter, perhaps in addition to the other processes resulting from exposure to a humorous stimulus, leads to reduction of tension because of the positive correlation between number of laughs and relaxation on the MACL.

With respect to HR change, the findings are less clear. On the one hand, the relationship between HR and humor is in the direction predicted by the hypotheses in all three tests. However, in two of these three tests, the relationship is not statistically significant. A cautious interpretation of these findings would be that the initial hypothesis that humor results in a decrease in HR was not supported. By the same token, and exercising the same level of caution, one must also state that the hypothesis that humor results in an increase in HR, as suggested by five earlier studies in this area, also fails to find support. From this viewpoint, the present findings do not demonstrate that any change in HR occurred.

In our judgment, such an interpretation would be excessively cautious. Since the initial theory was stated in terms of tension levels, rather than in terms of the two indices of tension, HR and MACL scores, the results should be interpreted in terms of the overall success of the theory. By this standard, the data support the theory, since the results were in the direction predicted in all six of the tests, an outcome exceedingly unlikely to occur by chance.

Given the modest size of the correlations, however, and the potential importance of some of the issues that have been raised, further research seems to be required before any definitive statement can be made about the relationship between humor and tension. One fruitful line of investigation would be to assess both the moment-to-moment and the net effects of laughter on HR. This procedure would allow one to assess the goodness of fit of the various models of catharsis described above: those of Berlyne, Gellhorn, and Scheff, as well as to test the theory of catharsis itself. Perhaps if observations of the amount of laughter were made (the number, duration, and intensity of laughs), the process, as well as the fact, of catharsis could be elucidated.

There is one further refinement that should be included in a subsequent study. Neither the present study, nor any of the earlier studies cited, investigated the duration of the net effects of humor. If humor causes net decreases in tension but these decreases are short-lived (as the elevations reported in the earlier studies seem to be), these findings would still be of considerable theoretical significance, in that they would increase our understanding of the relationships between emotional processes such as laughter and mental and physical states, such as mood and HR, respectively. They, however, would have little practical significance. If, on the other hand, the mental and physical changes caused by laughter were relatively long-lasting, they might have some immediate implications for practical matters of health, as well as theory. Two hypotheses that might be tested are: first, the momentary increase in HR caused by a laugh would be proportional to the duration and intensity of the laugh. Second, the duration of the net decrease in HR caused by a series of laughs would be related to the number, duration, and intensity of the laughs. To the extent that these two hypotheses were confirmed, the results would be of considerable theoretical and practical importance.

8.

Suggestions for Research and Applications

In this last chapter, I want to state the theory of distancing and catharsis in a formal way and examine its implications for future research. Before doing so, in order to illustrate the limitations of contemporary research on emotions, I will review the studies done in one particular context, the sociology of patient-staff interaction in medical settings. As it turns out, all of these studies are about emotion work. Zborowski's (1952) study of patients' responses to pain in terms of their cultural background is a case in point. According to the study, the patients of Jewish and Italian background summon up their feelings in response to pain, while the Yankee patients suppress them. In terms of the distancing paradigm, the Jewish and Italian patients are seen to be underdistanced from their feelings, the Yankee patients overdistanced.

Many of the studies concern medical personnel's socialization of feeling. Lief and Fox (1963) ("Training for detached concern in medical students") and Daniels (1960) ("Affect and its control in the medical intern") report how doctors are trained to suppress their feelings.

Studies of the nursing profession, such as those by Devereux and Weiner (1950) and by Schulman (1958), are about the conflicts nurses experience as they try to suppress their emotions and those of their patients. Schulman reports that the traditional role of the nurse is mother-surrogate, in which the expression and acknowledgment of emotion is the key feature. As nurses try to take on the role of dispassionate healer, they experience severe role conflict. All of these studies may be summarized as dealing with socialization of medical personnel to being over-distanced.

Finally, there are studies which describe staff-patient interaction, in which the key feature is the suppression of emotions. One well-known study, by Emerson (1970), on the pelvic examination ("Behavior in private places: sustaining definitions of reality in the gynecological examination") is about the suppression of embarrassment. Another study, by Glaser and Strauss (1965), reports the mutual pretense which surrounds the dying patient, whose main function seems to be the suppression of feeling. According to these studies, not only medical personnel, but patients as well, are socialized to be overdistanced from their feelings.

This brief review of studies of emotion in medical settings suggests some severe shortcomings, and how the use of the distancing paradigm might improve the quality of future research. The main consequence of my review is to highlight how descriptive and atheoretic these studies have been. All of the studies merely present a static picture of overdistancing, for the most part, in interaction or socialization. None of the studies shows, or even speculates about, the causes or consequences of the practices they describe. What processes give rise to the overdistancing of medical staff? To what extent are medical staff recruited to select persons who are already overdistanced in terms of their personality? To what *degree* are socialization and interaction overdistanced?

There is another entire set of questions dealing with the consequences of distancing. What are the consequences of overdistancing for medical staff? For patients' courses of illness? For their satisfaction with the kind of care they have received? The degree of overdistancing probably makes a great difference for the consequences. If the degree of overdistancing is mild, patients and staff might feel some awkwardness and tension in interaction, but there would probably be no long-range consequences. However, as the degree of overdistancing increased, we would hypothesize, according to the theory outlined in this book, that the effectiveness of treatment would decrease and the tension level of staff members would increase. At high levels of overdistancing we would hypothesize that treatment would become ineffective, whatever the technical skills of the staff, and their tension levels would increase to the point that they would be significantly affected in terms of job satisfaction and health.

The theory of distancing suggests that there should be a strong relationship between levels of emotional tension, amount of catharsis, and effectiveness of treatment. If tension levels are low, then treatment can be effective even if the amount of catharsis is minimal. But if tension levels are high, then the theory suggests the need for adequate catharsis for both patients and staff, if treatment is to be effective. Even if the illness is entirely physical, if it is severe enough it is always accompanied by distressing affects. Grief and fear, particularly, would seem to be virtually always present in severe illness. The theory of distancing suggests that these affects present a major problem in medicine.

In psychiatric medicine, distancing phenomena are at least as important as in physical medicine. One issue which needs to be investigated concerns those conditions which lead to rigidities in distancing regardless of the situation. It seems fairly clear that there are rigidities in distancing that are built into personality: most persons hold characteristic distances from their emotions. Shapiro (1965, 124–133) has typified the person characterized by "emotional outbursts or explosions" as having a *hysterical* personality style. I believe that Binstock (1973) mistakenly equates this style of emotionality with catharsis, since he does not distinguish between emotional distress and discharge. In terms of the theory of distancing, this style is characterized by underdistanced emotion, the vivid reliving of the emotional content of past traumas in the present. At the other extreme, Shapiro (23–54) refers to the *obsessive-compulsive* as, among other things, showing overcontrol of emotions. The person with this style " . . . *automatically* restricts not only affect experience, but also whim, playfulness, and spontaneous action in general" (44). He gives an example of laughing or excitement being experienced as loss of control of affect: " . . . a fear of 'losing control' is often experienced . . . when they start to laugh very hard or become unusually excited . . . " (p. 45). In terms of distancing, this personality style can be characterized as maintaining overdistancing from emotions and the routine and, indeed, automatic repression of emotions, both distress and discharge.

In a parallel way, the different psychotherapeutic doctrines also maintain the need for characteristic distance from emotions. Most contemporary doctrines are characterized by an overdistanced stance. Reality therapy and behavior modification are particularly overdistanced, and orthodox psychoanalysis, although less extreme, also emphasizes in actual practice more observation of, than participation in, past emotional states. At the other extreme, primal therapy seems completely underdistanced, in that it emphasizes the complete reliving of past emotional traumas, rather than a balance between participation and observation. Of all the major doctrines, only Gestalt seems to recognize the need for distancing and balance in emotional experience. Even in Gestalt, this concept is not clearly articulated.

The distancing paradigm suggests the need for a therapeutic doctrine which would stress balance in psychotherapy for both therapist and patient, rather than a rigid adherence to either overdistancing or underdistancing as always desirable. In the absence of an explicitly stated doctrine, perhaps a first approximation to optimal distancing could be obtained by matching patients and therapy in a compensatory way: overdistanced patients with an underdistanced therapy and vice versa.

A Formal Theory
The preceding chapters discuss ideas and concepts which imply a theory of catharsis, a theory that has not, as yet, been explicitly stated. At its simplest, a formal theory can be represented as a set of interrelated hypotheses. Although several hypotheses have been implied in the earlier chapters, a representation of the ideas in this book as a set of hypotheses may be an aid for further understanding and, particularly, might point toward further avenues of research and discussion. This last chapter presents a series of hypotheses which concern the interrelationships between emotional distress, repression, distancing, catharsis, and

other major concepts that have been discussed. The chapter ends with a discussion of some possible problems for future research.

In my role as a participant in cathartic therapies, and as a therapist who uses them, I am intimately acquainted with the processes that have been discussed here. I am accustomed to seeing and feeling the manifestations of distancing, for example, in my own life and in my practice of teaching and therapy: my training has led me to discern the differences in pitch, loudness, bodily tension, and gesture which may enable one to differentiate between expressions of grief at various distances. Laughing or crying at aesthetic distance has a relaxed and resonant quality, which is difficult to describe in words but is nevertheless often apparent in real life.

I am prefacing my discussion of a formal theory with these thoughts because of a difficulty I feel here in maintaining the requisite distance, as a writer, of being both an observer and a participant, more or less equally. A formal statement about catharsis and related processes, in the form of a series of hypotheses, feels much too distanced to me. The hypotheses seem to be totally from the outside: they seem like the work of an observer, rather than a participant, or even of a participant-observer. They seem, therefore, somewhat alien to my own experience. The narrative form of discourse, which has marked the preceding discussion, seems to me a more appropriate medium for conveying ideas about emotion, and about catharsis. In my experience, at least, a theory of catharsis should feel like an organic whole. The formal hypotheses chop it up, make it awkward and incomplete. With these apologies, I will now go about the business of stating hypotheses about catharsis, the conditions which lead to it or its absence, and its consequences.

Before stating the theory in terms of hypotheses, it will be useful to review the causes and consequences of catharsis in terms of temporal sequences which relate the major concepts that have been used. The cathartic process can be described in terms of the following sequence:

> 1a. Stress → 2. Distress → 3. Aesthetic distance →
> 4. Catharsis → 5. Assimilation → 6. Consequences

This sequence can be described as follows: environmental stress (1) leads to distress (2) or pain, which results in catharsis, (4) when the individual maintains optimal distance (3) from his or her distress, i.e., is equally a participant in and an observer of that distress. Under these conditions, the stimuli which gave rise to the experience of distress are assimilated (5) into the person's memory, and are available for future use, when needed, and the consequences (6) of the distressful experience and the resultant catharsis are positive, in terms of the person's perceptions, feelings, thought, and behavior. That is, after catharsis, the individual's sensitivities to the outside world and to his or her own inner stimuli are heightened, his or her feeling state is more pleasurable, his or her thoughts are clearer, and his or her behavior is more creative, than before or during catharsis. The process involving repression can be represented in a similar way:

> 1b. Stress → 2. Distress → 3. Over (under) distance →
> 4. Misstorage → 5. Consequences

Environmental distress leads to repression, rather than catharsis, if the distressful stimuli and/or the responding individual are not optimally distanced. That is, to the extent that the amount of stress is so great as to be overwhelming, in terms of intensity, frequency, and/or duration, or to the extent that the distressful stimuli are not adequately balanced by reassuring stimuli, or to the extent that the person involved is susceptible to the distressful stimuli, to that extent repression will occur.

In the event of repression, the distressful stimuli are not assimilated into one's experience so that they are routinely recallable. They are either seemingly forgotten, which is one manifestation of misstorage (4) or, as another manifestation of misstorage, they are reexperienced involuntarily (after a particularly upsetting scene, a participant may find that the scene may replay more or less continually in his or her consciousness, even though considerable effort is made to banish the disturbing thought).

Finally, the consequences of repression and misstorage lead to negative changes in perception, feeling, thought, and behavior. After emotions are aroused but not discharged, the individual's level of perceptual sensitivity is reduced, his or her feeling state is less pleasurable, thoughts are less clear and behavior less creative or more rigid.

These ideas concerning sequences can now be restated in the form of hypotheses which relate stages or conditions in a sequence:

1. Other things being equal, the greater the stress, the greater the distress. The more the amount of stress, in terms of frequency, intensity, and duration, the greater emotional distress for the individual. For example, the more frequently and the longer period of time an infant is separated from the parent, the more distress, in the form of grief, he or she experiences. The stress can be in the form of danger, frustration, boredom, loss of face, or any combination of these.

2(a). Other things being equal, the greater the distress, the more likely that repression will occur. One of the principal conditions for repression involves the massiveness of the stressful conditions; to the extent that the individual is overwhelmed by stress, the resulting distress is likely to be repressed. Another condition, however, concerns interpersonal emotion work, rather than the amount of stress. This hypothesis must be qualified in two ways, see 2(b) and 2(c) below. First, some provision must be made for the individual's susceptibility to distress.

2(b). The more punitively discharge is socialized, the more repression will occur.

2(c). To the extent that an individual has accumulated emotional distress in an area, to that extent the magnitude of stress required to cause repression in that area is diminished. For example, an infant who has experienced frequent unresolved losses will become more susceptible to grief, and each subsequent experience of separation will lead to further repression. Tomkins (1963) refers to this cycle as the "snowball" model of psychological distress. Emotional distress associated with a particular stimulus appears to interfere with the individual's ability to discriminate stimuli in that area, but at the same time, the ability to generalize stimuli is unimpaired.

2(d). The more the accumulated distress in an area, the cruder will be the resemblance of new stimulus to the original stimulus, required to cause repression.

3(a). To the extent that the individual experiences emotional distress at optimal distance, catharsis will occur. Distancing acts to decrease the relationship between the amount of stress and the amount of repression. To the extent that emotional distress is caused by stressful stimuli balanced by reassuring stimuli (e.g., separations that occur in a context of continuing attachments, or danger that occurs in a context of safety), catharsis will occur. Again, this hypothesis needs to be qualified in terms of the individual's ability to experience catharsis.

3(b). To the extent that the individual is repressed in an area, to that extent an excess of reassuring stimuli over stressful stimuli will be required to insure catharsis.

In terms of the consequences of repression and catharsis, our discussion has suggested a relationship between these two variables and consequences for thought, feeling perception, and behavior.

4(a). The more repression associated with a given type of stimulus, the lower the intelligence; the less positive and the more tense the state of feeling, the more insensitive the perceptual abilities and the more rigid the behavior. This hypothesis can also be stated in a positive form, in terms of the amount of catharsis or distress.

4(b). The more the catharsis in a given area, or the less distress, the greater the intelligence, the more positive and less tense the feeling state, the more sensitive the perceptual abilities and the more flexible the behavior in that area. A similar hypothesis can be stated with respect to social solidarity.

4(c). The more the repression, the more isolated the individual, which has a corollary at the societal level:

4(d). The more the repression, the less social solidarity.

The amount of therapeutic change is related to the amount of catharsis; but it is also related to other considerations. First of all, there is usually at least some emotional distress accumulating in the course of everyday life. Second, the amount of change is inversely related to the absolute level of repressed emotion. These considerations may be expressed, for purposes of discussion, as an equation with the following form:

5. Improvement in the state of feeling (Improvement-F) is a function of the amount of catharsis (C) over a given period of time, less the amount of distress (D) accumulated over the same period of time, divided by the level of repressed emotion (L):

$$\text{Improvement-F} = \frac{C - D}{L}$$

Improvement in behavior (Improvement-B) involves the same considerations, as well as others. Changes in behavior are determined not only by changes in the level of repressed emotion, but also by cognitive and perceptual reintegration of dissociated material.

6. Change is a function, therefore, of the ratio of the amount of reintegration (Ir), which is an expression of the process of "working through," and of the level of cognitive insight, to the level of dissociation. The equation would be:

$$\text{Improvement-B} = \frac{C - D}{L} \frac{Ir}{\text{Diss.}}$$

These equations are heuristic only, since the concepts have not been operationally defined. Together with the other hypotheses, they represent some of the major processes postulated in the theory of catharsis.

Directions for Research

From the standpoint of empirical research, the most crucial distinction made in this discussion is between emotional distress and emotional discharge, processes which are not differentiated in most studies. For example, Lazarus (1966) presented a film showing several highly distressing events (crude surgery on the genitals of native Australian tribal women) to three different audiences. In the first audience, the sound track emphasized the "trauma" (the mutilation and danger of disease), in the second, the sound track encouraged denial, stressing the harmlessness of the procedure and the eager expectancy of the participants, and the third intellectualized the whole affair, offering a detached anthropological perspective. The results of these different presentations would be easily interpretable in terms of the theory of catharsis: the first should lead to an underdistanced response from the audience, since both film and sound were distressful. The second might lead to a mixed state, since the film was distressful, but the sound track denied any distress. The result might be an overdistanced state in the audience. Finally, the third presentation might lead to discharge, since the sound track did not deny distress, but sought to put it in an emotionally and morally meaningful frame. However, since Lazarus did not make any distinction between distress and discharge (he showed that the mean galvanic skin response was different in each of the three groups but did not interpret the significance of the differences), his results cannot be evaluated in terms of the actual effects of the treatment stimulus on the viewers.

What is needed are psychophysiological studies of fear, grief, anger, and embarrassment which would include reliable measures of tension (both subjective and objective measures) on the one hand, and amount of discharge on the other. The study of laughter reported in Chapter 7 provides an example. Similar studies should be conducted for the emotions of fear, grief, and anger. Moreover, future studies should determine not only the short-term effects of catharsis, as the Scheff-Scheele study did, but also long-term effects.

For example, a study of children's television viewing might compare the effects of viewing violent fare with the effects of situation and cartoon comedy on tension levels. I would hypothesize that regular viewing of violence increases tension levels, and regular viewing of comedy, to the extent that it gives rise to laughter, decreases tension levels, both on a short-term and long-term basis. Such studies might help end the impasse now existing over the impact of television viewing on children. Almost all of the existing studies try to determine what effect the viewing of violence has on violent behavior. One source of ambiguity in these studies is that violent behavior is a relatively rare event, which is not readily observable by researchers. Another problem is that all of these studies control only for the type of stimulus (i.e., violence versus non-violence), none control for, or measure, the amount of distancing or catharsis. The projected study would remove these problems, since the amount of catharsis would be systematically measured and since tension level is an easily measured, directly observable, dependent variable.

Another study that is needed concerns the distinction Nichols and Zax make between cognitive catharsis, the detailed recall of forgotten events, and somatic catharsis, laughing and crying, etc. Under what conditions, and with what effects, does each type of catharsis occur? As already indicated, I hypothesize that in the case of deeply repressed emotion, lengthy episodes of repeated somatic catharsis occur before cognitive catharsis, which signals the last phase of the catharsis process, can occur. The exception to this hypothesis is in the case where there is a single type of repressed emotion, boredom or stimulus deprivation. In this case, all of the catharsis will take the form of cognitive catharsis.

Still another area of needed research concerns the operational measurement of the distancing of emotional response. Aesthetic distancing implies a process of participation in and observation of repressed emotion, of being able to move back and forth freely between the distress of an overwhelming emotional event and the safety and reassurance of the present moment, whether that moment is occurring in therapy, ritual, or theatre. My definition of aesthetic distance at this point relies heavily on subjective measures: the participant's feeling of control over the discharge process, of being able to exercise at least partial control over starting it, and, especially, stopping it, should it become unbearable. Objective measures are implied in my definition, however, and need to be studied. Body posture, direction of gaze, gestures, and, especially, facial expression can be recorded and rated systematically to determine whether attention is being directed in or out. It may be that high-speed motion picture photography will be needed to catch the micromomentary changes in facial expression that are hypothesized to accompany catharsis at aesthetic distance.

The discussion of the Schachter-Singer (1962) study implied the need for a replication, since the results of the study have been interpreted in a way that is critical for our basic assumptions about the nature of emotions. In the replication I envision, it will be necessary to study the effects of physiological, cognitive, and social determinants of emotional reactions, as was done in the original study, but at varying levels of emotional intensity, which was not done. Suppose that one could induce a mild, moderate, and strong response by varying the amount of the drug used. I would hypothesize that the cognitive and social determinants play a smaller role, and the physiological determinants a larger role, with increasing intensity. One would also need to measure and compare systematically emotional expression in the different social contexts, as well as including a control group, which the original study failed to do.

For research and clinical purposes, it would be useful to develop a scale which provided a reliable measure of the amount of emotional distress and discharge characterizing an individual. Distress might be indexed by questions about characteristic tension levels, frequency of nightmares and slips of the tongue, obsessions or compulsions, and levels of discharge by establishing norms of frequency, intensity, and duration of crying, shivering, laughing, etc., for men and women.

Preliminary interviews and questionnaires given to several hundred college men and women have led me to believe that there are considerable differences between them in how frequently and intensely they experience catharsis. My impressions are that the great majority of men in American society rarely discharge grief; crying of any kind is infrequent, of short duration, and low in intensity. Women presented a quite different picture: crying was frequent, of long duration and great intensity among the majority. It seemed to me, however, that a considerable amount of the crying reported, perhaps as much as one-quarter, was marked by the signs of underdistancing (lack of relief, feelings of pain, defeat, hopelessness, tension, and lack of control) and with sequels of discomfort such as headache and swelling and redness in the eyes.

A similar but much less marked difference concerning fear occurred in the groups studied. The feeling of fear was reported by women more frequently than by men. But few of either group reported ever experiencing the discharge of fear, i.e., shivering and sweating in a situation of danger in which there is a feeling of control and pleasure, which in turn brings relaxation and mental clarity. A somewhat greater number of women than men reported the discharge of fear. My impressions with respect to grief and fear were that men are much more repressed in these two areas than women, and women discharge grief much more than men, and fear, somewhat more.

The situation with anger and embarrassment was reversed in the groups I studied. In these two areas, women were more repressed than men, and discharged less. In both groups, the majority frequently felt angry, but displays of anger were much more frequent among the men. As in the case of women's crying, however, much of the expression of anger reported by the men (more than half) was marked by signs of underdistancing: feelings of loss of control and lack of resolution and relaxation. It was interesting that expressing anger appears to mean different things to men and to women. Men frequently described physical expressions such as fighting, yelling, and slamming doors. Women frequently reported verbal expression, silence, withdrawal, and sarcasm as their conceptions of the expression of anger.

Frequency, duration, and intensity of laughter is related to the expression of both anger and embarrassment. The majority of both groups reported great frequency of laughter, although more men laughed and at greater frequency. If one looks only at intense laughter or laughter of long duration, there was a much larger difference between the two groups. Few women reported ever "belly laughing" or having fits or jags. In contrast, most men reported having such experiences frequently. Belly laughing and laughing fits or jags are more reliable signs of cathartic laughing than reports of simple laughter, which could involve social laughter (which may be quite overdistanced) or tense laughter (which is likely to be a manifestation of underdistanced embarrassment or anger). It would therefore appear that men discharge much more embarrassment or anger

219

through laughter than women. Women subjects frequently volunteered that belly laughs or laughing fits or jags were "unladylike."

These preliminary results suggest that the stereotype of men as much less emotional (Balswick and Peek, 1976, 55–77) or more emotionally "constipated" (Farrell, 1974) is extremely inaccurate. A more accurate description would be that men are more repressed with respect to grief and fear, and women, with respect to anger and embarrassment. Perhaps of equal importance are the similarities between the sexes. Although the findings suggest that the majority of women frequently discharge grief and the majority of men frequently discharge embarrassment or anger through laughter, neither group appears to do very well with fear or rage. A systematic survey of these behaviors and feelings could be used to establish standards for constructing a distress-discharge scale, as well as beginning a more substantive kind of research on the emotional dynamics connected with sexual roles.

A distress-discharge scale would be useful in studying the emotional dynamics of large-scale organizations. Organizations can be distinguished by the amount of verbal and emotional information that is conveyed in intraorganizational communication. Shibutani (1961, 164) has called attention to the finding reported in studies of aphasia (loss of ability to use words) and Parkinson's disease (where there is loss of ability to express emotion) that it is easier to understand a person suffering from aphasia than one having Parkinson's disease. Apparently meaning can be communicated by gesture, even without language. But when no emotions are expressed, one cannot tell how the speaker feels about what he or she is saying, leaving a vacuum of understanding.

If one could differentiate organizations on the basis of the amount of internal verbal and emotional communication, these measures might predict important organizational features. I would hypothesize that organizations high on verbal communications but low on emotional communication, which might be called Parkinsonian organizations, would show high levels of tension, low job satisfaction, high rates of turnover, short-term efficiency, and long-term inefficiency. Such organizations would be characterized by precise coordination of behavior but would lack social solidarity. Members would know what other members were doing but not how they felt about what they were doing. I would guess that such organizations would make few errors, but the errors that were made would be large ones.

Organizations with low rates of verbal communication and high rates of emotional communication would be characterized by low levels of tension, high job satisfaction, low rates of turnover, short-term inefficiency, and long term efficiency. Such an organization, which might be called the aphasic type of organization, would lack precision in coordination but would have a high level of social solidarity. There would be some confusion about what other members were doing but widespread knowledge about motives and feelings. Such an organization would be characterized by frequent but correctable mistakes.

I would further hypothesize that in modern societies, the Parkinsonian organizations far outnumber the aphasic ones. There are many, many Sparky Andersons (the martinet coach of the Detroit Tigers baseball team) for every Tommy Lasorda of the Dodgers. In Parkinsonian organizations in industry, the military, and government, there may be an association between leadership and the overdistancing of emotion. Harland Svare, former coach of the San

Diego professional football team, has been quoted as explaining his decision to accept the job of head coach in this way: "[Before taking the job] it's like I've been in neutral. Things have been beautiful but dull. . . . I just couldn't feel completely alive. I need a challenge that involves a lot" (Mandell, 1976, 59).

The feeling of dullness, of not being completely alive, is one of the marks of overdistancing. Svare goes on to formulate a theory of leadership based on his own experience:

> . . . I've noticed that the difference between the biggies and the [others] is not just IQ or how much dough they have behind them. It's also how quick they get bored. I mean, how quick and strong new things have to come to make them feel alive. [One has] got to move on to bigger things faster in order not to feel dead. He has to get into more and bigger danger, or nothing is happening. He has to have stronger stuff right away to avoid the emptiness of nothing. . . . The people who desperately need more and more . . . action, get to the top . . . of companies, teams, armies, what have you (ibid., 61).

Svare's idea can be restated as a hypothesis that overdistancing is the source of participation in hazardous sports, like hang gliding and skydiving, and of the leadership of large-scale organizations. It would be possible to test this hypothesis by administering the distress-discharge scale to individuals at the different levels of leadership in a large organization. If the hypothesis is correct, the higher the position the greater the level of distress and the less the discharge, both because Parkinsonian organizations select such persons for leadership, and the situation of leadership, in turn, creates more distress and fewer opportunities for discharge.

Another project using a distress-discharge scale would seek to establish the mechanism of the transmission of emotional repression through socialization of children by their parents. An investigation of patterns of distress and discharge in a sample which spanned three generations (children, their parents, and their grandparents) would use questions about the way each individual's emotions were socialized by his or her parents and how that individual, in turn, socialized the emotions of his or her children, in addition to the questions on the distress-discharge scale. The hypothesis to be tested would be that the more distressed the individual, the more punitively the emotions of the children of that person will be socialized.

Studies of separation protest in infants (crying and screaming when the mother leaves) could be used to study a similar problem using techniques of observation, rather than survey. Kagan and his collaborators (1976) have found that the extent of separation protest varies from culture to culture; for example, the majority of the African Bushmen babies in their sample began protest at an early age (between five and ten months), and ended late (about thirty months), while the majority of the Guatemalan Indian babies began late (between ten and fifteen months) and ended early (about fifteen months). In these studies, however, there is no attempt to specify the causes of this variation or its consequences. My hypothesis would be that the variation is caused by differential socialization: the Bushmen parents use reward socialization and the Guatemalan parents use punishment. Furthermore, these differential practices should have observable consequences for the personality of the children: the Bushmen practice should result in expressive and flexible individuals, the Guatemalan practice in inexpressive and rigid individuals. An alternative hypothesis would be that the Bushmen babies cry more than the Guatemalan babies because they undergo more loss and pain. The observed differences would be accounted for not by differences in socialization but by differences in the intensity and amount of distress the babies encounter. These issues would require empirical study to unravel.

A source of study of emotional discharge in natural settings may be found in children's games and recreations. Spontaneous games which give rise to laughter (tongue-twisters) or fear (hide-and-seek) might be studied for their effects on tension levels. Similarly, children who ride roller coasters or other thrill rides might also be expected to show fear discharge and reduction of tension after rides.

The study by Symonds of the causes of success in psychotherapy should be replicated. Such a study would require a formal, operational definition of catharsis, such as the one offered here or its equivalent, in order to correct some of the deficiencies in the original study. Such a study would be especially helpful if it were done in conjunction with the use of a distress-discharge scale similar to the one mentioned above, with incoming patients. A question which Symonds did not ask, but which would also expand the study, would concern the issue of repeated catharsis on the same distressful event. Is such repetition necessary? If so, is the repetition exactly the same, or, as Freud conjectured, does it concern differing facets of the same experience? This issue is related to the question of the "therapeutic facsimile" (Moreno, 1971). Psychodrama may begin with a real situation but usually is modified to make it more effective. These modifications are probably governed by application of various distancing techniques of the kinds discussed in earlier chapters, but clinical examples might show additional techniques that are effective.

Further studies of the consequences of discharge are probably necessary. The study reported in Chapter 7 established that catharsis reduces tension, but the theory specifies other consequences that need to be studied. Koestler argues that creativity is a consequence of laughing and crying, which is also suggested by the theory outlined in Chapter 3. A study which determined levels of intelligence or creativity, before and after measured amounts of catharsis, should be necessary to test this hypothesis. (For a first step in this direction, see Soderberg, 1972). The theory also specifies that increases in social solidarity should be a consequence of collective catharsis, an important hypothesis for political sociology. Such a hypothesis could be tested by interviewing groups concerning their commitment to and liking for the group before and after various kinds and intensities of collective catharsis.

The processes through which music and dance lead to emotional arousal and catharsis are little understood and might prove valuable for understanding mechanisms of distancing and catharsis. The relationship between the rhythms of music and biological rhythms such as the beat of the heart is one direction that might be examined. Another starting place for investigation is Meyer's (1956) analysis of why a minor key is heard in Western countries as being sad, but is heard differently in countries of the Middle East.

The field of medicine offers a number of promising areas for research on catharsis. Since Doust and Leigh (1953) found such striking evidence relating the cessation of asthma symptoms to catharsis, a replication of their study would seem very much needed. Another phenomenon which might be productively investigated is the relationship between hypertension and laughter and other forms of catharsis. The study in Chapter 7 showed that brief periods of laughter led to reduction of heart rate. One implication of this finding is that it might be possible to reduce heart rate and blood pressure by having individuals change their television viewing habits, by reducing the underdistanced fare (violence, suspense, etc.) and increasing the optimally distanced fare (comedy, classical drama).

One application of the theory offered here would be to seek to modify existing ritual or mass entertainment in a way that allows more catharsis in the audience, as indicated in Chapter 5. Relatively minor increases in distance, introduced by having more discrepant awareness, stylization, and/or comic relief in film and television fear dramas, should increase audience catharsis substantially. Another direction would be the creation of new social forms which allowed catharsis, by combining ritual, entertainment, therapy, political, or communal functions. The trend toward individually tailored marriage ceremonies, which are more meaningful to the bride and groom than the traditional ceremony, seems to be a step in this direction. Perhaps such social inventions would require far more knowledge about distancing, and more confidence in the effectiveness of catharsis, than we presently have. If further research produces the knowledge and the confidence, the invention of new cathartic forms might then become a goal of the highest priority.

Bibliography

Alexiou, Margaret. 1974. *The Ritual Lament in Greek Tradition*. Cambridge, Eng.: Cambridge University Press.

Aristotle. 1968. *Poetics*. D. W. Lucas (ed.). Oxford, Eng.: Clarendon Press.

Arnheim, R. 1971. *Entropy and Art*. Berkeley: University of California Press.

Averill, James R. 1968. "Grief: Its nature and significance." *Psychological Bulletin* 70: 721–748.

———. 1969 "Automatic response patterns during sadness and mirth." *Psychophysiology* 5: 399–414.

Ax, A. F. 1953. "The physiological differentiation between fear and anger in humans." *Psychosomatic Medicine* 15: 433–442.

Balswick, Jack O., and Charles W. Peek. 1976. "The inexpressive male: A tragedy of American society," in D. S. David and R. Brannon (eds.), *The Forty-Nine Percent Majority*. Reading, Mass.: Addison-Wesley.

Barber, C. L. 1959. *Shakespeare's Festive Comedy*. Princeton, N.J.: Princeton University Press.

Belden, Jack. 1949. *China Shakes the World*. New York: Monthly Review Press.

Benedict, Ruth. 1934. *Patterns of Culture*. New York: Mentor.

Berkowitz, Leonard, 1962. *Aggression: A Social Psychological Analysis*. New York: McGraw-Hill.

———. 1970. "Aggressive humor as a stimulus to aggressive responses." *Journal of Personality and Social Psychology* 16: 710–717.

Berlyne, D. E. 1971. *Aesthetics and Psychobiology*. New York: Appleton-Century-Crofts.

———. 1972. "Humor and its kin." In J. H. Goldstein and P. E. McGhee (eds.), *The Psychology of Humor*. New York: Academic Press.

Binstock, W. A. 1973. "Purgation through pity and terror." *International Journal of Psychoanalysis* 54: 483–504.

Blumer, Herbert. 1946. *Principles of Sociology*. New York: Barnes and Noble.

Booth, Wayne C. 1961. *The Rhetoric of Fiction*. Chicago: University of Chicago Press.

Borquist, Alvin. 1906. "Crying." *American Journal of Psychology* 17: 149–205.

Bowlby, John. 1969. *Attachment and Loss. 1. Attachment*.

———. 1973. *Attachment and Loss. 2. Separation: Anxiety and Anger*. London: Hogarth.

Bozzuto, James C. 1975. "Cinematic neurosis following 'The Exorcist.'" *Journal of Nervous and Mental Disease* 161: 43–48.

Branch, A. Y., G. A. Fine, and J. M. Jones. 1973. "Laughter, smiling, and rating scales: An analysis of responses to tape recorded humor." Reprinted from the Proceedings, 81st Annual Convention, APA.

Bullogh, Edward. 1912. "Psychic distance as a factor in art and an aesthetic principle." *British Journal of Psychology* V: 669–679.

Candland, Douglas K., et al. 1977. *Emotion*. Monterey, Calif.: Brooks/Cole.

Cannon, W. B. 1927. "The James-Lange theory of emotions: a critical examination and an alternative theory." *American Journal of Psychology* 39: 106–124.

Chapman, Anthony J. 1975. "Humorous laughter in children." *Journal of Personality and Social Psychology* 31, 1: 42–49.

Chapman, Anthony J., and Hugh C. Foot. 1976. *Humor and Laughter*. London: Wiley.

Chapple, Eliot D. 1970. *Culture and Biological Man: Explora-*

tions in Behavioral Anthropology. New York: Holt, Rinehart and Winston.

Cousins, Norman. 1976. "The anatomy of an illness (as perceived by the patient)." *New England Journal of Medicine* 295 (26): 1458–1463.

Cupchik, G. C., and H. Leventhal. 1974. "Consistency between expressive behavior and the evaluation of humorous stimuli: The role of sex and self-observation." *Journal of Personality and Social Psychology* 30: 429–442.

Daniels, M. 1960. "Affect and its control in the medical intern." *American Journal of Sociology* 66: 259–267.

Devereux, G., and F. R. Weiner. 1950. "The occupational status of the nurse." *American Sociological Review* 15: 628–634.

Dirks, J. F., et al. 1978. "Panic-fear in asthma: Rehospitalization following intensive longterm treatment." *Psychosomatic Medicine* 40 (Feb.): 5–13.

Douglas, Mary. 1970. *Natural Symbols.* London: Barrie and Jenkins.

Doust, John W. L., and Denis Leigh. 1953. "Studies on the physiology of awareness: The interrelations of emotions, life situations, and anoxemia in patients with bronchial asthma." *Psychosomatic Medicine* 15: 292–311.

Dunbar, Helen Flanders. 1954. *Emotion and Bodily Changes.* New York: Columbia University Press.

Durkheim, Emile. 1961. *The Elementary Forms of the Religious Life.* New York: Collier.

Dworkin, E. S., and J. S. Efran, 1967. "The angered: Their susceptibility to varieties of humor." *Journal of Personality and Social Psychology* 6: 233–236.

Ekman, Paul, and Wallace Friesen. 1969. "Non-verbal leakage and cues to deception." *Psychiatry* 32: 88–106.

Ekman, Paul, Wallace Friesen, and Phoebe Ellsworth. 1972. *Emotion in the Human Face.* New York: Pergamon.

Ellenberger, Henri. 1970. *The Discovery of the Unconscious.* New York: Basic Books.

Emerson, J. 1970. "Behavior in private places: sustaining definitions of reality in gynecological examinations." Pp. 74–97 in H. P. Dreitzel (ed.), *Recent Sociology #2.* New York: Macmillan.

Engel, George L. 1971. "Sudden and rapid death during psychological stress." *Annals of Internal Medicine* 74 (May): 771–782.

Evans, Bertrand. 1960. *Shakespeare's Comedies*. London: Oxford University Press.

Evans-Pritchard, E. E. 1965. *Theories of Primitive Religion*. Oxford, Eng.: Clarendon Press.

Farrell, Warren. 1974. *The Liberated Man*. New York: Random House.

Feshback, Seymour and Jerome Singer. 1971. *Television and Aggression*. San Francisco: Jossey-Bass.

Figge, Horst H. 1975. "Spirit possession and healing cult among the Brasilian Umbanda." *Psychotherapy and Psychosomatics* 25: 246–250.

Firth, Raymond. 1951. *Elements of Social Organization*. London: Henry E. Walter.

———. 1972. "Verbal and bodily rituals of greeting and parting." Pp. 1–38 in J. S. LaFontaine (ed.), *Interpretation of Ritual*. London: Tavistock.

Foxe, Arthur N. 1941. "The therapeutic effect of crying." *Medical Record* (March 5): 167–168.

Frank, Jerome. 1961. *Persuasion and Healing*. Baltimore: Johns Hopkins University Press.

French, Thomas M. 1939. "Psychogenic factors in asthma." *American Journal of Psychiatry* 96: 89.

Freud, Sigmund. 1905. *Jokes and Their Relationship to the Unconscious*. New York: Norton (1960).

———. 1910. *Five Lectures on Psychoanalysis*. London: Hogarth.

———. 1948. *Collected Papers*. Translated by Joan Riviere. London: Hogarth.

———. 1949. *A General Introduction to Psychoanalysis*. New York: Perma Giants.

———. 1961. *Beyond the Pleasure Principle*. New York: Norton.

Freud, Sigmund, and Joseph Breuer, 1895. *Studies on Hysteria*. New York: Avon Books (1966).

Fry, W. F. 1963. *Sweet Madness: A Study of Humor*. Palo Alto, Calif.: Pacific Books.

———. 1969. "Humor in a physiologic vein." *News of Physiological Instrumentation*. Beckman Laboratory.

————, and P. E. Stoft. 1971. "Mirth and oxygen saturation levels of peripheral blood." *Psychotherapy and Psychosomatic Medicine* 19: 76–84.

Fuchs, Stephan. 1964. "Magic healing techniques among the Balahis in Central India." Pp. 121–138 in Ari Kiev (ed.), *Magic, Faith and Healing*. New York: Free Press.

Funkenstein, Daniel H., S. H. King, and M. E. Drollette. 1957. "Perceptions of parents and social attitudes." in P. Hock and J. Zubin (eds.). *Experimental Psychopathology*. New York: Grune and Stratton.

Garrison, Webb. 1971. "Tears and Laughter." *Today's Health* (March) 29–32.

Geen, Russell G. 1976. "Observing violence in the mass media: Implications for basic research." Pp. 193–234 in Russell G. Geen and Edgar C. O'Neal (eds.), *Perspectives on Aggression*. New York: Academic Press.

Geertz, Clifford. 1965. "Religion as a cultural system." Pp. 204–216 in William A. Lessa and Evons Z. Vogt (eds.), *Reader in Comparative Religion*. New York: Harper and Row.

Gellhorn, Ernest, and G. N. Loofbourrow. 1963. *Emotions and Emotional Disorders*. New York: Hoeber.

Glaser, Barney, and Anselm Strauss. 1964. "Awareness contexts and social interaction." *American Sociological Review* 29: 669–679.

Goddard, Harold C. 1951. *The Meaning of Shakespeare*. Chicago: University of Chicago Press.

Godkewitsch, M. 1976. "Physiological and verbal indices of arousal in rated humor." In A. J. Chapman and H. C. Foot (eds.), *Humor and Laughter: Theory, Research, and Applications*. London: John Wiley.

Goffman, Erving. 1956. "Embarrassment and social organization." *American Journal of Sociology* 62: 264–274.

————. 1959. *Presentation of Self in Everyday Life*. Garden City, N.Y.: Anchor.

————. 1971. *Relations in Public*. New York: Harper and Row.

————. 1974. *Frame Analysis*. New York: Harper and Row.

Gorer, Geoffrey. 1965. *Death, Grief, and Mourning*. Garden City, N.Y.: Doubleday.

Graham, O. T. and S. Wolf. 1950. "Pathogenesis of urticaria." *Psychosomatic Medicine* 13: 122.

Greenson, Ralph R. 1967. *The Technique and Practice of Psychoanalysis.* Vol. 1. New York: International Universities Press.

Greenwald, H. 1975. "Humor in psychotherapy." *Journal of Contemporary Psychotherapy* 7: 113–116.

Grinker, Roy R. 1953. *Emotions and Emotional Disorders.* New York: Hoeber.

Gross, Edward, and Gregory P. Stone. 1964. "Embarrassment and the analysis of role requirements." *American Journal of Sociology* 70: 1–15.

Haggard, E. A., and F. S. Isaacs. 1966. "Micromomentary facial expressions as indicators of ego mechanisms in psychotherapy." Pp. 154–165 in L. A. Gottschalk and A. H. Averback (eds.), *Methods of Research in Psychotherapy:* New York: Appleton-Century-Crofts.

Harbage, Alfred. 1947. *As They Liked It.* New York: Macmillan.

Heilbrunn, Gert. 1955. "On weeping." *Psychiatric Quarterly* 24: 245–255.

Heusner, A. Price. 1946. "Yawning and associated phenomena." *Physiological Review* 26: 156–168.

Himmelweit, Hilde T. 1958. *Television and Children.* Oxford, Eng.: Oxford University Press.

Hinton, John. 1967. *Dying.* London: Penguin.

Hinton, William. 1966. *Fanshen.* New York: Vintage.

Hochschild, Arlie. 1975. "The sociology of feeling and emotion: Selected possibilities." Pp. 280–307 in Marcia Millman and Rosabeth M. Kanter (eds.), *Another Voice: Feminist Perspectives on Social Life and Social Science.* Garden City, N.Y.: Anchor.

———. "Sex Differences in the Culture of Emotion: A Study of the Relation Between Self and Feeling." Unpublished manuscript.

Holland, Norman H. 1964. *Psychoanalysis and Shakespeare.* New York: McGraw-Hill.

Holloway, John. 1961. *The Story of the Night.* Lincoln: University of Nebraska Press.

Honigmann, E. A. J. 1976. *Shakespeare: Seven Tragedies: The Dramatist's Manipulation of Response*. London: Macmillan.

Huntington, W. R. 1973. "Death and the social order: Bara funeral customs (Madagascar)." *African Studies* 32: 65–84.

Izard, Carroll. 1971. *The Face of Emotion*. New York: Appleton-Century-Crofts.

Jackins, Harvey. 1965. *The Human Side of Human Beings*. Seattle: Rational Island.

James, William. 1890. *The Principles of Psychology*. New York: Holt.

Janov, Arthur. 1970. *The Primal Scream*. New York: Dell.

Jephcott, E. F. N. 1972. *Proust and Rilke: The Literature of Expanded Consciousness*. London: Chatto and Windus.

Jones, Ernest. 1953. *The Life and Work of Sigmund Freud*. Vol. I. New York: Basic Books.

Jones, J. M. and P. E. Harris. 1971. "Psychophysiological correlates of cartoon appreciation." *Proceedings of the Annual Convention of the American Psychological Association* 6: 381–382.

Kagan, Jerome. 1976. "Emergent themes in human development." *American Scientist* 64: 186–196.

Kaplan, Robert M. and Robert D. Singer. 1976. "Television violence and viewer aggression: A reexamination of the evidence." *Journal of Social Issues* 32: 18–34.

Karle, W., et al. 1973. "Psychophysiological changes in abreactive therapy: Study 1, primal therapy." *Psychotherapy: Theory, Research, and Practice* 10: 117–122.

Katz, Richard. 1973. "Education for transcendence: Lessons from the !Kung Zhu/Twasi." *Journal of Transpersonal Psychology* 5: 136–154.

Klapp, Orrin E. 1969. *Collective Search for Identity*. New York: Holt Rinehart and Winston.

Kluckhohn, Clyde. 1942. "Myths and rituals: A general theory." *Harvard Theological Review* 35: 45–49.

Knapp, Peter H., and S. J. Nemetz. 1957. "Sources of tension in bronchial asthma." *Psychosomatic Medicine* 19: 466.

Koestler, Arthur. 1964. *The Act of Creation*. New York: Dell.

Kubie, L. S. 1970. "The destructive potential of humor in psychotherapy.'' in W. Mendel (ed.), *A Celebration of Laughter*. Los Angeles: Mara Books, 67–80.

Lacey, Beatrice C., and John I. Lacey. 1974. "Studies of heart rate and other bodily processes in sensorimotor behavior." Pp. 538–564 in Paul A. Obrist et al. (eds.), *Cardiovascular Psychophysiology*. Chicago: Aldine.

Lain Entralgo, Pedro. 1970. *The Therapy of the Word in Classical Antiquity*. New Haven: Yale University Press.

Langevin, R. and H. I. Day. 1972. "Physiological correlates of humor." Pp. 129–142 in J. H. Goldstein and P. E. McGhee (eds.), *The Psychology of Humor*. New York: Academic Press.

Lazarus, Richard. 1966. *Psychological Stress and the Coping Process*. New York: McGraw-Hill.

Lee, Richard B. 1968. "The sociology of !Kung bushmen trance performances." Pp. 34–35 in Raymond H. Prince (ed.), *Trance and Possession States*. Montreal. R. M. Bucke Memorial Society.

Lesser, Simon O. 1957. *Fiction and the Unconscious*. Boston: Beacon Hill Press.

Lévi-Strauss, Claude. 1969. *The Raw and the Cooked*. New York: Harper and Row.

Liebert, Robert M. and Neala S. Schwartzberg. 1977. "Effects of mass media." *Annual Review of Psychology* 28: 141–173.

Lief, H., and R. C. Fox. 1963. "Training for detached concern in medical students." Pp. 12–35 in H. Lief (ed.), *The Psychological Basis for Medical Practice*. New York: Harper and Row.

London, Harvey, Daniel S. Schubert, and Daniel Washburn. 1972. "Increase of autonomic activity by boredom." *Journal of Abnormal Psychology* 80:29–36.

Lowenfeld, John. 1961. "Negative affect as a causal factor in the occurence of repression, subception, and perceptual defense." *Journal of Personality* 29: 54–63.

Lucas, D. W. (ed.). 1968. *Aristotle's* Poetics. Oxford: Clarendon Press.

Lynd, Helen M. 1958. *On Shame and the Search for Identity*. New York: Harcourt, Brace.

Mack, Maynard. 1962. "Engagement and detachment in Shakespeare's plays." Pp. 275–297 in Richard Hosely (ed.), *Essays on Shakespeare and Elizabethan Drama*. Columbia: University of Missouri Press.

Malinowski, Bronislaw. 1945. *Magic, Science, and Religion*. Glencoe, Ill.: The Free Press.

Mandelbaum, David G. 1959. "Social uses of funeral rites." Pp. 189–217 in Herman Feifel (ed.), *The Meaning of Death*. New York: McGraw-Hill.

Mandell, Arnold J. 1976. *The Nightmare Season*. New York: Random House.

Martin, L. 1905. "Psychology of esthetics: Experimental prospecting in the field of the comic." *American Journal of Psychology* 16: 35–116.

Masters, William, and Virginia Johnson. 1966. *Human Sexual Response*. Boston: Little, Brown.

Maurer, Adah. 1967. "The game of peek-a-boo." *Diseases of the Nervous System* 28: 118–121.

Mendel, W. 1970. *A Celebration of Laughter*. Los Angeles: Mara Books.

Meyer, Leonard B. 1956. *Meaning and Emotion in Music*. Chicago: University of Chicago Press.

Mindess, H. 1956. *Laughter and Liberation*. Los Angeles: Nash.

Modaressi, Tahi. 1968. "The Zar cult in South Iran." Pp. 149–155 in Raymond H. Prince (ed.), *Trance and Possession States*. Montreal: R. M. Bucke Memorial Society.

Moreno, J. L. 1971. "Psychodrama." Pp. 460–500 in H. I. Kaplan and B. J. Sadock (eds.), *Comprehensive Group Psychotherapy*. Baltimore: Williams and Wilkins.

Mullan, Sean, and Wilder Penfield. 1959. "Illusions of comparative interpretation and emotion." *AMA Archives of Neurology and Psychiatry* 81 (March): 269–284.

Nichols, Michael P. 1974. "Outcome of brief cathartic psychotherapy." *Journal of Consulting and Clinical Psychology* 42: 403–410.

Nichols, Michael P., and Melvin Zax. 1977. *Catharsis in Psychotherapy*. New York: Gardiner Press.

Nowlis, V. 1965. "Research with the mood adjective checklist." Pp. 352–389 in S. S. Tomkins and C. Izard (eds.), *Affect, Cognition, and Personality*. New York: Springer.

Obeyesekere, Gananath. 1970. "The idiom of demonic possession: A case study." *Social Science and Medicine* 4: 97–111.

Obrist, P. A. et al. 1974. "The cardiac-somatic interaction." Pp. 136–162 in P. A. Obrist et al. (eds), *Cardiovascular Psychophysiology*. Chicago: Aldine.

O'Dea, Thomas F. 1970. *Sociology and the Study of Religion*. New York: Basic Books.

Oswald, Peter F. and Philip Peltzman. 1974. "The cry of the human infant." *Scientific American* 230: 84–91.

Penfield, Wilder, and Lamar Roberts. 1959. *Speech and Brain Mechanisms*. Princeton: Princeton University Press.

Penfield, Wilder, and P. Perot. 1963. "The brain's record of auditory and visual experience." *Brain* 86: 595–696.

Perksky, H. et al. 1958. "Relation of emotional responses and changes in plasma hydrocortisone level after a stressful interview." *Archives of Neurology and Psychiatry* 79: 434–447.

Pincus, Lily. 1974. *Death and the Family: The Importance of Mourning*. New York: Vintage.

Plutchik, Robert. 1954. "The role of muscular tension in maladjustment." *Journal of General Psychology* 50: 45–62.

Pollio, H. R., R. Mers, and W. Lucchese. 1972. "Humor, laughter, and smiling: some preliminary observations of funny behaviors." Pp. 211–239 in J. H. Goldstein and P. E. McGhee eds.), *The Psychology of Humor*. New York: Academic Press.

Pollock, G. 1972. "On mourning and anniversaries: The relationship of culturally constituted defense systems to intrapsychic adaptive processes." *The Israel Annals of Psychiatry and Related Disciplines* 10: 9–40.

Proust, Marcel. 1978. *Remembrance of Things Past*. New York: New American Library (1934).

Pulver, Sydney. 1971. "Can affects be unconscious?" *International Journal of Psychoanalysis* 52: 347–354.

Quanty, Michael B. 1976. "Aggression catharsis: Experimental investigations and implications." Pp. 99–132 in Russell G. Geen and Edgar C. O'Neal (eds.), *Perspectives on Aggression*. New York: Academic Press.

Radcliffe-Brown, A. R. 1952. *Structure and Function in Primitive Society*. Glencoe, Ill.: The Free Press.

Rosenblatt, Paul C. et al. 1976. *The Expression of Emotion in Bereavement*. New Haven: HRAF Press.

Rosenzweig, S. 1936. "Some implicit common factors in diverse methods of psychotherapy." *American Journal of Orthopsychiatry* 6: 412–415.

Rothbart, Mary K. 1973. "Laughter in young children." *Psychological Bulletin* 80: 247–256.

Sadoff, Robert L. 1966. "On the nature of crying and weeping." *Psychiatric Quarterly* 40: 490–503.

Sargant, William. 1974. *The Mind Possessed*. Philadelphia: J. B. Lippincott.

Sattler, Jerome M. 1966. "Embarrassment and blushing: A theoretical review." *Journal of Social Psychology* 69: 117–133.

Saul, Leon J. and C. Bernstein, Jr. 1941. "The emotional setting of some attacks of asthma." *Psychosomatic Medicine* 3: 349.

Schachter, Stanley and David Singer. 1962 "Cognitive, social and physiological determinants of emotional state." *Psychological Review* 69: 379–399.

Scheff, Thomas J. 1972. "Reevaluation counseling: social implications." *Journal of Humanistic Psychology* 12: 58–71.

———. 1977. "The distancing of emotion in ritual." *Current Anthropology* 18: 483–505.

Schneider, Louis. 1970. *Sociological Approach to Religion*. New York: John Wiley.

Schulman, S. 1958. "Basic functional roles in nursing: Mother surrogate and healer." Pp. 528–537 in E. G. Jaco (ed.), *Patients, Physicians and Illness*. Glencoe, Ill.: Free Press.

Seitz, P. F. 1951. "Symbolism and organ choice in conversion reactions." *Psychosomatic Medicine* 13: 254–259.

Selye, Hans. 1956. *The Stress of Life*. New York: McGraw-Hill.

Shapiro, David. 1965. *Neurotic Styles*. New York: Basic Books.

Shibutani, Tamotsu. 1961. *Society and Personality*. Englewood Cliffs, N.J.: Prentice-Hall.

Singer, D.L. 1968. "Aggression arousal, hostile humor, catharsis." *Journal of Personality and Social Psychology*. Monograph Supplement 8, 1–14.

Smelser, Neil. 1963. *Theory of Collective Behavior*. New York: Free Press.

Smith, Adam. 1975. *Powers of the Mind*. New York: Random House.

Soderberg, Paul L. 1972. "The effects of control-free emotional behavior on attention." Ph.D. dissertation, USIU, San Diego, Calif.

Southard, L. D. and M. Katahn. 1967. "The correlation between self-reported and mechanically recorded pulse rates." *Psychosomatic Science* 8: 343–344.

Stark, Rodney, and Charles Y. Glock. 1968. *American Piety*. Berkeley: University of California Press.

Stearns, F. R. 1972. *Laughing: Physiology, Pathology, Psychology, Pathopsychology and Development*. Springfield, Ill.: Charles C. Thomas.

Swift Arrow, Bernadine. 1974. "Funeral rites of the Quechan tribe." *The Indian Historian* 7: 22–24.

Symonds, Percival. 1954. "A comprehensive theory of psychotherapy." *American Journal of Orthopsychiatry* 24: 697–712.

Tomkins, Silvan S. 1963. *Affect/Imagery/Consciousness*. Vol. II. New York: Springer.

Turner, Ralph. 1976. "The real self: From institution to impulse." *American Journal of Sociology* 81: 989–1016.

Turner, Ralph H. and Lewis M. Killian. 1957. *Collective Behavior*. Englewood Cliffs, N.J.: Prentice-Hall.

Turner, Victor. 1967. *The Forest of Symbols*. Ithaca, N.Y.: Cornell University Press.

Volkan, Vamik D. 1975. "Re-grief therapy." Pp. 334–350 in Bernard Schoenberg et al. (eds.), *Bereavement: Its Psychosocial aspects*. New York: Columbia University Press.

Weiner, Herbert. 1977. *Psychobiology and Human Disease*. New York: Elsevier.

Wimsatt, W. K., Jr. and C. Brooks. 1957. *Literary Criticism*. New York: Random House.

Woolf, Virginia. 1976. *Moments of Being*. London: Harcourt Brace Jovanovich.

Zborowski, M. 1952. "Cultural components in responses to pain." *Journal of Social Issues* 8: 16–30.

Zigler, E., J. Levine, and L. Gould. 1967. "Cognitive challenge as a factor in children's humor appreciation." *Journal of Personality and Social Psychology* 6: 332–36.

Index of Names

Index of Names

Subject Index

Subject Index

of response, 13, 66–67, 105–106
of stimulus, 66–67
of violence, 24–25, 141–42
techniques of, 106–108, 134–140,
  147–148, 156–170
distress, emotional, 49, 145–146,
  211, 212
  as contrasted with emotional
    discharge, 50, 58, 74–75, 80,
    101
  evoked by mass entertainment,
    125–128

ego, splitting of the, 60
embarrassment, 54–55, 56
  cathartic process of, 48, 56, 65
emotion(s)
  at aesthetic distance, 61, 65
  biological function of, 10–12
  complex, 49
  in social theory, 3–8
  over-distanced (repression), 61, 63,
    65
  relation to thought and behavior,
    6–8, 51–53, 160
  "social emotion", 12
  social psychology of, xiii
  unconscious, 52, 56n, 62–64
  under-distanced, 61
  undifferentiated, 3–4
emotion work, 8–9, 10, 204–205

fear
  cathartic process of, 48, 57–58, 65,
    123–124
  distress of, 49, 50, 54, 57
female role and emotion, 64–65,
  218–220
"files," the, 34–35
fixation, 42 (see also rigidity)

games, children's, xii, 115–116,
  130–34
Gestalt therapy, xii, 21, 47, 208
grief, 53–54, 58–59, 99–100
  cathartic process of, 48, 58, 65, 123

heart rate, 184–188, 190, 198–201
hysteria, 27–28, 30, 33
  cause of, 33–36, 41 .
  Freud's and Breuer's treatment of,
    38–39, 41
hysterical style, 207

inclusion-exclusion, social, 156
insight, 21, 103–104
instinct, 11, 47, 54

jealousy, 64–65

laughter, 15–16, 24, 48, 50, 59, 65,
  67, 68, 69, 75, 83, 102, 130,
  132–133, 136, 141, 142–143,
  159–161, 183–203, 216,
  218–220, 224–225
linking objects, 77
loss, 53–54, 54n, 56, 58
love, 53–54, 56

male role, 20, 64–65, 218–220
mourning, 20, 22, 121–123

obsessive-compulsive style, 207
orgasm, sexual, 56–57

participant-observation (aesthetic
  distance), 61–63, 119
participant-observer balance, xiv,
  216–217
Primal therapy, 21, 78, 87
psychoanalysis, 21

re-evaluation
  counseling (RC), x-xi, xii, 48, 60
  process of, 53
reflex, 47
regrief therapy, 22
Reichian therapy, 47
remembering, 69
repressed emotion
  return of (under-distanced emotion),
    63, 65, 125–127
repression, 33–34, 36–37, 53,
  117–118, 129–130, 204–205,
  210–211, 212–213
  consequences of, 51–53
re-stimulation, 61
rigidity, 14, 17–18
ritual
  management of emotional distress,
    115–116, 130–134
  poverty of, 120, 128–130
  relationship to catharsis, 21
rolfing, xii

schizophrenia diagnosis, 18
sentiments, 4

245

Subject Index

Designer:	Carolyn Bean Associates
Compositor:	Typesetting Services of California
Printer:	Vail-Ballou Press, Inc.
Binder:	Vail-Ballou Press, Inc.
Text:	VIP Times Roman
Display:	VIP Cooper Black
Cloth:	Joanna Arrestox B14550
Paper:	55 lb. Antique Cream